Auditing Oracle E-Business Suite: Common Issues

ISBN # 978-1-329-52976-2

Published by ERP Risk Advisors

ERP Risk Advisors
Greeley, CO 80633
United States

Phone 970-785-6455
http://www.erpra.net

Oracle is a registered trademark of Oracle Corporation

Other trade and service marks are the property of their respective owners.

Order additional copies at http://www.lulu.com/spotlight/jeffreythare

About the Author

Jeffrey Hare's extensive background includes public accounting (including Big 4 experience), industry, and Oracle Applications consulting experience. He has been working in the Oracle Applications space since 1998 with implementation, upgrade, and support experience. His main focus is on the development of internal controls and security best practices for organizations running Oracle Applications. Jeffrey is a Certified Public Accountant (CPA), a Certified Information Systems Auditor (CISA), and a Certified Internal Auditor (CIA).

He has written various white papers and articles, some of which have been published by organizations such as ISACA, the ACFE, and the OAUG. Jeffrey has worked in various countries including Australia, Austria, Canada, Mexico, Brazil, United Kingdom, Ireland, Panama, Saudi Arabia, Germany, and the United Arab Emirates. Jeffrey is a graduate of Arizona State University and lives in northern Colorado with his wife and three daughters. You can reach him at jhare@erpra.net.

Table of Contents

Acknowledgements

I'd like to thank the following professionals for your input on the content of this book, my first book, and the various white papers which have formed the foundation for this book:

Stephen Kost, Daryl Geryol, Craig O'Neill, Michael Scott, and Mike Miller.

I'd also like to thank my three daughters, Allie, Caelyn, and Becca who are amazing young ladies. I am blessed to be your dad and can't wait to see how God uses you.

Finally, I'd like to thank my wife, Julie. You are the love and my life and an amazing partner. God has blessed me with a Proverbs 31 woman and I can't imagine doing life without you.

Dedication of Proceeds

100% of the proceeds of this book will be given to a charity that is focused on helping children who have been trafficked or are at risk for human trafficking. The organization is a Christ-centered charity called Rapha House. Find out more about this organization as www.RaphaHouse.org.

The mission of Rapha House is to love, rescue, & heal children who have been rescued from trafficking & sexual exploitation. Given that I am the father of three girls, the work of this organization is near to my heart.

Foreword

So much to write about and so little time. I love to write and have to pick and choose my battles, so to speak…

After much thought about what to write next, I thought this book would be most valuable to the broader community. I will hopefully be able to make small tweaks to it without feeling like I have to spend weeks on end to complete an update.

If you have comments or questions about the content or have a query you'd like me to consider adding, please don't hesitate to contact me at jhare@erpra.net.

ERP Risk Advisors hosts the industry's most subscribed to public domain listserver related to internal controls and security issues for Oracle Applications. I suggest you sign up for this listserver and encourage your colleagues to as well at: http://tech.groups.yahoo.com/group/OracleSox/ (originally set up as a listserver to focus on Sarbanes-Oxley compliance and has since been broadened to deal with internal controls and security best practices regardless of compliance requirements).

If you are an end user, I encourage to you sign up for the Internal Controls Repository (ICR) at (https://groups.yahoo.com/neo/groups/oracleappsinternalcontrols/info). The ICR is a repository that shares practical content such as forms personalization specs, sample policies, standards, and procedures, and other content related to internal controls and security. The ICR is limited to end users only because I share some of my most valuable Intellectual Property (IP) in that forum. Other firms and end user organizations have provided content as well for me to share with others through the ICR. This content, as well as content shared by others, is also published in the public domain listserver described above (OracleSox).

What Makes This Book Different

I have been performing GRC health checks on many types of companies of varied sizes for years and have noticed many of the 'basics' aren't being addressed. Over and over I see the same issues in these assessments. So, rather than trying to write a book that addresses everything, I decided to write a book that addresses the most common issues I see and which have significant risk to an organization running Oracle E-Business Suite.

This book is different from other books in that it is practical and very detailed. Most of the issues I highlight in this book can be addressed and evaluated through a series of SQL queries that I and others have developed. My goal in this first release isn't to cover every risk a company can possibly face, but to address certain high risk areas often passed over by companies. Subsequent versions of this book will continue to evolve the content.

Who Should Read this Book

This book is written specifically with the IT auditor in mind. This version is written to give internal auditors and external auditors the tools needed to perform a 'basic' audit – to be completed somewhere in the range of 10 to 30 hours. I suspect internal auditors at organizations running Oracle E-Business Suite will also want to use the material in this book to stay ahead of external auditors as they adopt this material for their audits.

Contact Information

If you have comments or questions on any information in this book or other books in this series, don't hesitate to send me an email at jhare@erpra.net.

Chapter 1: Introduction

One of the most difficult parts about writing a book like this is to decide the scope. Inevitably, what I include and don't include will leave just about everyone disappointed in some respect.

This book is designed to be read with at least a 'basic' understanding of Oracle's security model. As such, I recommend having either of my other books handy as well. My first book "Oracle E-Business Suite Controls: Application Security Best Practices" would be sufficient to gain this basic understanding. As of the publishing of this book, I am also working on a major revision to that book which will be titled "Oracle E-Business Suite Controls: Foundational Principles". The new book will also cover the fundamentals needed to understand for the material in this book and more.

That new book is designed for auditors, internal and external, to use as a basis for evaluating the fundamentals of IT General Controls (ITGCs) also referred to as General Computing Controls (GCCs).

My goal is to continue to evolve this book with new SQL queries and a broader Internal Controls Questionnaire to address relevant risks for organizations running Oracle E-Business Suite.

Visit erpra.net to get the latest set of SQL queries so you don't have to re-type them. Choose the 'Books' link and you will find a Word document with the queries and the Internal Controls Questionnaire.

To help you understand when I am addressing specific functionality within the application, I have made the words upper case. For example, when I am talking specifically about Users form I use the upper-case Users. When I am talking generically about users (people) of the applications, I use the word in lower-case. This is particularly important when referring to responsibilities a user may perform as opposed to Responsibilities assigned to a User.

Another comment to set the tone of the book… I have not addressed Roles at all in this first edition of the book. A significant portion of the risk related to application security can be addressed by looking at Responsibilities without have to look at Roles (in the User Management context). I used the term 'roles' often in a generic sense. The essence of role-based access control (RBAC) standards I cover in my first book in detail. RBAC principles, in summary, mean you create access for a system based on the role (job functions) a person or group of people perform for an organization. In most organizations, the use of the User Management module is unnecessary, except in very limited circumstances. In the areas where it is required to be used, the risks are relatively small.

Remember, I am starting with the premise that the intent of this book isn't to address ALL risks, but to provide an audit program for the most common risks I have seen that are not being addressed at all or are being poorly addressed. As time goes on, I intend to add other material to this book. Maybe someday it will be complete.

Chapter 2: Audit Program

I have seen and evaluated many different Audit Programs over my career. There are a variety of structures and approaches to developing an audit program. Rather than try to pick one structure that I believe encompasses the best of all I have seen, I am providing a basic audit program and letting the reader build these concepts into the structure best fitting your organization or firm.

Thus, I am not going to tie the audit steps, risks, or controls to any control framework. I'll leave that for you to do. One of the objectives of those frameworks (COSO, Cobit, ITIL, etc.) is to provide a structure to achieve completeness in your assessment or audit. My goal in this book is not to provide a complete audit, but to fill in certain gaps that I have seen over the years. As such, the content is not 'complete'. It should be used to supplement existing audit programs your firm or organization is already using to audit Oracle E-Business Suite.

Following is summary:

Test #	Audit Test Summary
OV-1	Password decryption risk
OV-2	Compliance with Secure Configuration Guide
OV-3	Role design
OV-4	Generic Users – Vendor
OV-5	Generic Users – Custom
OV-6	Stale Users
OV-7	Disabling accounts related to Terminated Users
OV-8	AZN menus
OV-9	Use of seeded Responsibilities
OV-10	High risk profile options
OV-11	Profile options risk assessment
OV-12	User profile values
OV-13	System profile values
OV-14	Access to high risk concurrent programs
OV-15	Chart of accounts maintenance
OV-16	Password policy - expiration date
OV-17	Password policy compliance

Test #	Audit Test Summary
OV-18	Access to sensitive administrative pages and forms
OV-19	Excessive access to Alert Manager
OV-20	Excessive access to IT functions
OV-21	Instance strategy
OV-22	Configuration Change Management policy
OV-23	Excessive access to configurations subject to the Change Management process
OV-24	Employees with more than one User

Each of these steps will be documented in detail. Each audit step will contain a Risk and Control Description along with the Testing Procedure. If you identify issues as part of the testing procedures, I have presented language that you could use to present the 'Finding' in the following format:

- Observation
- Risk
- Recommendation
- Level of Effort
- Priority

I have used this format in various assessments I have performed. I expect you will likely use a reporting format appropriate for your organization.

I use the following categorization of Level of Effort and Priority to help provide further context for the Finding. This helps management evaluate the effort necessary to fix the issue and how important the issue is to remediate.

Level of Effort

Estimates based on our understanding of the effort needed to make the changes are as follows:

- High – represents a significant effort by Acme Co. that would include multiple resources, a structured project, and project management oversight. These activities would take weeks or months in total, taking into consideration planning, execution, and oversight.

- Medium – represents activities that should probably take less than a month perhaps as little as a few days.
- Low – represents activities that should probably take from as little as a day or two to only a few minutes.

Priority

- Critical – finding represents an extreme security risk and should be corrected as quickly as possible. Some of these are low effort.
- High – finding represents a significant security risk and should be corrected within a few months.
- Medium – finding in which risk is not critical, but correction should be implemented within the next year.
- Low – finding in which the risk is relatively low and could addressed when it is convenient. Recommendations identified are an enhancement and which don't pose a security risk are rated as low. Some of these, however, could be combined with the more sensitive risks.

A caveat I use related to Priority is as follows:

ERPRA has classified the priority as best as possible based on observations, the functionality, and an understanding of the operating environment of Acme Company. Acme Company should review and confirm or change the priority based on your own risk assessment. Acme Company should also thoroughly test the solutions and apply necessary and appropriate change management processes before migrating them to Prod.

Chapter 3: OV-1 Password Decryption Risk

OV-1: Password decryption risk

Background:

Oracle introduced in 11.5.10 RUP 6 and 12.0.4 a process to migrate Oracle Applications User passwords to a non-reversible hash password scheme. Don't assume the new non-reversible hash password scheme has been applied to your environment just because you have upgraded from 11i to an R12 point release or if you've completed a fresh install of an R12 point release. We have audited instances where we were certain the FNCPASS Utility process had been run only to be surprised that it hadn't been.

Find out more about this issue in Oracle's MOS Note: 457166.1.

Risk:

Application User passwords may be decrypted and multiple other User accounts may be used to circumvent application controls. Additionally, the 'APPS' password could be decrypted allowing full access to DML and DDL privileges in the Production instance.

Control Description:

Organization has applied the patch to change the way passwords are stored to the hashing method according to MOS Note 457166.1.

Testing procedure:

Query 13: Password patch

Comments related to testing:

Testing should be straight forward. The script returns the results. If the result is the patch hasn't' been applied, then you have a finding.

Possible Finding language:

Following is potential language to document your finding:

Observation:

Organization has not applied the process recommended in MOS Note 403537.1 to migrate to non-reversible hash passwords. Page 22 of that Note makes the following recommendation:

SWITCH TO HASHED PASSWORDS

Traditionally Oracle E-Business Suite has stored the password of the application users (FND_USERS) in encrypted form. Starting with 12.0.4 it is possible to switch the EBS system to store hashed versions of the passwords instead.

To switch EBS to use hashed passwords you must use the FNDCPASS command line utility in MIGRATE mode, see MOS Note 457166.1 "FNDCPASS Utility New Feature: Enhance Security With Non-Reversible Hash Password", for the actual command and a list of client/server components that will need an update to work with hashed passwords.

Risk:

Failure to migrate to the non-reversible hash password scheme leaves application and database passwords vulnerable to being decrypted. To find out more about the vulnerabilities, search "Integrigy application password decryption white paper" and you will find a white paper written by Integrigy, a partner firm of ours, entitled "Oracle Applications 11i Password Decryption."

Following is a summary of steps necessary due to the failure to migrate to hash passwords:

1. VERIFY APPLSYSPUB DOES NOT HAVE ACCESS TO FND_USER_VIEW
2. CHANGE GUEST ACCOUNT PASSWORD
3. CHANGE PASSWORDS FOR ALL SEEDED ORACLE APPLICATIONS ACCOUNTS
4. CHANGE PASSWORDS FOR ALL DATABASE ACCOUNTS
5. CREATE ALL NEW APPLICATION ACCOUNTS WITH STRONG PASSWORDS
6. SET SERVER SECURITY TO SECURE
7. IMPLEMENT MANAGED SQL*NET ACCESS
8. LIMIT ACCESS TO FND_USER AND FND_ORACLE_USERID
9. CHANGE ALL APPLICATION ACCOUNT PASSWORDS DURING CLONING

10. CHANGE THE GUEST ACCOUNT PASSWORD DURING CLONING
11. CHANGE ALL DATABASE ACCOUNT PASSWORDS DURING CLONING

Recommendation:

Follow the steps recommended in 403537.1 to migrate to hashed passwords.

Level of Effort:

High

Priority:

Critical

Chapter 4: OV-2 Compliance with Security Configuration Guide

OV-2 - Compliance with Secure Configuration Guide

Background:

I always say that compliance with this document is mandatory, but it is not complete. Oracle has not done a good job of updating this document on a regular basis. There was one period of time where it hadn't been updated in four and a half years, an eternity in the context of technology risk. I and others have consistently found flaws or instances where the document is incomplete. My observation is that it appears maintenance of this document hasn't been a part of the release process.

I'd recommend you read an article I wrote on this topic called "With Oracle Sometimes You Need to Fill in the Blanks". You can access this article at www.erpra.net.

There are dozens of steps to be followed in this document covering risks at the following levels: application, database, application server, operating system, and network. I often find that there is not an awareness of this document by my client. If the response to the ICQ is that they are aware of it and have implemented the recommendations, other procedures will be able to verify these statements. We typically find issues with OV-4 (Generic Users), OV-10 (High risk profile options), and OV-18 (Sensitive Admin pages).

Risk:

There are dozens of risks associated with lack of compliance with this document. Some examples are:

- Unapproved access to forms and pages that allow SQL injection or OS scripts to be executed through them
- Generic users being utilized for application maintenance
- Corruption of the database through back door access to maintain internal 'id' columns
- System performance issues
- Unsecured database logins

- Excessive data growth
- Changes being made outside the change management policy (i.e. unapproved changes)

Control Description:

Organization is knowledgeable of Oracle's "Secure Configuration Guide for Oracle E-Business Suite" (MOS Note 403537.1 for R12 and 189367.1 for 11i). Organization has followed the recommended steps in this guide. For the recommended steps that the organization hasn't followed, organization has documented the reasons why, the related risks, and has had management sign off on the acceptance of such risks.

Testing procedures:

The primary test of this control is the ICQ. However, there are some specific tests I have included in this book. To the extent that these specific tests have findings, you could document an overall finding that this document needs to be reviewed as a whole.

- Internal Controls Questionnaire (ICQ)
- OV-4: Generic Users – Vendor
- OV-10: High risk profile options
- OV-18: Access to sensitive administrative pages and forms

Comments related to testing:

If one or more of these tests fail, it would provide evidence that at least a portion of this document hasn't been followed.

There are other SQL statements provided by Oracle that could be used to verify some of the other recommendations in this MOS Note. I have included some 'bonus' scripts in the document on our website in the file containing the SQL scripts. These are scripts from Oracle that could be used to identify other steps that haven't been followed and which aren't addressed in this book.

Possible Finding language:

Following is potential language to document your finding:

Observation:

Organization is not in compliance with many of the recommendations from Oracle's "Secure Configuration Guide for Oracle E-Business Suite Release 12" (MOS Note 403537.1). Several examples are:

- AZN menus are available to users to access high risk functions
- Not monitoring activity of forms and pages that allow SQL injection or Operating System scripts
- Not disabling seeded users
- Inappropriate setting of the following profile options:
  - Utilities: Diagnostics
  - FND: Diagnostics (Other specific profile options...)

Risk:

There are dozens of risks associated with lack of compliance with this document. Examples are:

- Unapproved access to forms and pages that allow SQL injection or OS scripts to be executed through them
- Generic users being utilized for application maintenance
- Corruption of the database through back door access to maintain internal 'id' columns
- System performance issues
- Unsecured database logins
- Excessive data growth
- Changes being made outside the change management policy (i.e. unapproved changes)

Recommendation:

ERPRA recommends a team lead by IT (with help from the functional users) evaluate and document compliance with this MOS Note.

ERPRA recommends an evaluation be performed by an independent firm that specializes in E-Business Suite security assessments.

Level of Effort:

High

Priority:

Critical

Chapter 5: OV-3 Role design

Background:

I could write a whole book about this topic. My goal here isn't to detail everything that could go wrong with respect to role design, but to identify key issues which are typically wrong in role design and which are fairly easy to test through inquiry or through a few scripts. The proper way to test role design is through a SaaS service or installed software that tests role design risks (commonly referred to as 'SoD software).

At a high level, consider the following standards related to role design:

- Follow the principle of 'least privilege'
- Grant access to enable a user to fulfill a job function
- Limit access to sensitive data
- Minimize risks related to sensitive functions
- Minimize risks related to segregation of duty conflicts

Following are detailed expectations based on these principles:

- Generally, the goal is to design a single responsibility for each role in the organization. This can be accommodated where the access is limited to modules that are Operating Unit or Inventory Access based – such as Purchasing, Payables, Receivables, and Cash Management. Other common modules use different security models and generally should be segregated into their own Responsibility – Assets, and General Ledger. Each role should have a custom Menu and a custom Request Group which reflects the role requirements and which is based on the principle of least privilege (i.e. has no more and no less than what is necessary to perform their job function).

Most often security is developed module by module, with pseudo-sub-roles being developed for each module. The net result is Users end up with multiple Responsibilities in the same module rather than a single Responsibility for a given module (or group of modules where they can be combined). This may cause inefficiencies in daily activities because Users need to switch Responsibilities.

- Configurations (primarily in the Setup menu for each module) have been evaluated as to risk. Those that should be subject to the change management process have been identified and assigned to just those that are authorized to make the changes in Prod. I prefer each module has a specific Configuration responsibility with only those Functions subject to the change management process.

- Development of changes is segregated from the moving of such changes to the Test (for user acceptance testing) and Production. This includes object-oriented changes as well as changes that are made through the forms or pages in the Application (configurations, security changes, etc.)

- IT is only granted access in Prod to the business processes which the Process Owner authorizes them to make changes. Generally for mature organizations, such access is very limited, often only to Inquiry access in Prod. Never are IT users granted access to a Super User responsibility in Prod that would give them ability to override controls and cause Segregation of Duties issues

- Access is built from the ground up, even lower risk Functions are not assigned in Prod. This is, in part, to reduce auditors from requiring 'lookbacks' during audits. Even configurations which aren't being used, such as SLA setups, may be identified by external auditors as impacting one or more application controls. Therefore, unless explicitly needed, access to a form or page should not be assigned to anyone in Prod. As new functionality or modules are identified to be used, access is then granted to the roles (and therefore users) that are authorized to change the data.
- All application maintenance is done through a named login unless the vendor explicitly requires a specific login to be used and such login has permissions that can't be replicated by a named login. This is the case with the use of SYSADMIN in a few cases.

- Scheduling of concurrent programs is done through a custom generic login that only has the ability to schedule jobs and doesn't have the ability to enter or maintain data through any forms or pages.

Risk:

Excessive access to high risk single functions, excessive access to sensitive data, and segregation of duties violations. These risks could lead to fraud, theft or exposure of sensitive data, overriding controls, and misstatements in the financial statements.

Control Description:

Roles are designed based on Role Based Access Control and principle of least privilege concepts.

Testing procedures:

Query 1: Active Responsibility Definitions

Query 2: Active Users and their Assigned Responsibilities

Query 12: High Risk Single Functions

Comments related to testing:

If you are looking to test access to specific functions, query 12 could be used. However, the limitation of query 12 (doesn't take into account Menu and Function exclusions) is significant and means extensive testing using query 12 isn't feasible.

To properly test role design, the best method is to use software. I have built content to test role design and have licensed it exclusively to CaoSys to use in their SaaS solution (CS*Proviso) and their installed solution (CS*Comply). The content is, by far, the most comprehensive rule set to test the three legs of the stool – segregation of duties, high risk single functions, and access to sensitive data.

Contact me at jhare@erpra.net if you want more information related to these options.

Chapter 6: OV-4 Generic Users - Vendor

Background:

Refer to Oracle MOS Note 403537.1 for details of the recommendations related to these vendor-supplied generic users. As with any changes, make sure you test thoroughly the disabling of these accounts before making these changes in Prod.

In the MOS document, related to SYSADMIN it says "Do not disable the SYSADMIN user account until you have created other accounts with similar privilege." My experience is that SYSADMIN can't be disabled as it impacts workflow processes.

Risk:

Application maintenance (configurations, master data, or transactions) by a generic account that potentially obfuscates the person performing the maintenance.

Control Description:

Vendor-supplied generic application users are properly managed and monitored according to vendor's recommendations and organizations policy. Where recommendations by vendor do not exist, organization has analyzed risks related to such users and put in appropriate controls. This typically means disabling of accounts, where possible, reducing the access for such accounts to a minimum, requiring usage of such accounts to be justified and logged, and monitoring the usage of such accounts where they remain active.

Testing procedure:

Query 4: Generic Users

Comments related to testing:

When analyzing the results of Query 4, recognize that some Users have to remain active (GUEST and SYSADMIN) at all times. Other Users have to remain active only if certain modules are being used. Typically, I find one or more Users active that can be disabled.

Possible Finding language:

Following is potential language to document your finding:

Observation:

Four seeded logins provided by Oracle as stated by Oracle in MOS Note: 403537.1

- OP_CUST_CARE_ADMIN
- OP_SYSADMIN
- ASGADM
- APPSMGR

Risk:

Application maintenance (configurations, master data, or transactions) by a generic account may potentially obfuscate the person performing the maintenance.

Recommendation:

Inactivate all Users that can be disabled. See recommendations in Oracle's My Oracle Support note 403537.1. Typically, all can be disabled other than SYSADMIN and GUEST unless you use one or more applications that require the use of the login to run the application. Make sure you disable the logins in a non-production environment and perform extensive regression testing to confirm standard functionality, application extensions, or customizations are not impacted by the disabling of the account.

For users that cannot be disabled such as GUEST and SYSADMIN, these users should not be end-dated, but their activity should be tracked. This would include minimizing responsibilities assigned to these users, monitoring responsibility assignments (or removal of end-dated for disabled responsibilities), having any login of SYSADMIN be justified by logging the activity in your change management system, reconciling actual logins to such activity, reviewing SignOn Audit Login data for these users, and monitoring unsuccessful logins. SYSADMIN should only have System Administrator and User Management assigned to it and should only be used where required by an Oracle patch. In all other cases, users should use their named login in conjunction with a System Administrator responsibility rather than the SYSADMIN login. See full recommendations in our book in the chapter related to controls over Users. For GUEST, follow recommendations in Oracle's My Oracle Support Note # 443353.1.

Level of Effort:

Low

Priority:

High

Chapter 7: OV-5 Generic Users – Custom

Background:

In this chapter we are addressing generic users set up by the organization (i.e. custom) as opposed to those in the prior chapter which are 'seeded' or supplied by Oracle as part of the installation of the applications. The function of the most common type of generic custom User is for job scheduling. I sometimes see significantly more access assigned to these generic users than is really necessary, such as sometimes assigning "Super User" responsibilities because organizations believe such access is necessary to schedule jobs. However, in reality often all that is needed is the ability to submit requests ("Requests: Submit") and a well-designed Request Group. See a specification for this on the Book Resources page at our website.

Risk:

Application maintenance (configurations, master data, or transactions) by a generic account may potentially obfuscates the person performing the maintenance.

Control Description:

Custom generic application users are properly developed and monitored. This typically means developing access according to the principle of least privilege, requiring usage of such accounts be justified and logged, and monitoring the usage of such accounts.

Testing procedure:

- Query 2: Users and Assigned Responsibilities
- Query 8: Possible Generic Users

Comments related to testing:

This one is a bit trickier to test since we have to identify the generic users rather than knowing them from the beginning like those provided by Oracle. I look at the results of two queries to try to identify these custom users. The first is Query 2 which identifies all active Users and their active assigned Responsibilities. For this query, I prepare a pivot table with Users summarized. Then I scan through the list looking for any anomalies in the names of the Users. Sometimes you'll find Users with 'Sched' or 'PCT' contained in them or Users named "INTERFACE" "CONVERSION" or "CONCURRENT". When you combine the analysis with the results of Query 8 you have a higher chance of confirming if a User is generic.

Query 8 identifies Users that don't have an employee associated with the login. If your organization uses Human Resources or at least enters employees so that workflow hierarchies are built, an employee is associated with a User. In the situation where you expect all Users to have an employee associated with them, a User without an employee associated with it may indicate a generic User. If it is a generic User, you'd know it is a custom User (rather than a seeded or vendor-supplied User) because it doesn't show up in OV-4 (Query 4: Generic Users).

Possible Finding language:

Following is potential language to document your finding:

Observation:

CONCURRENT User appears to be a custom generic user and has significant access in Prod. CONCURRENT is assigned the following high risk Responsibilities. Such Responsibilities are excessive since a job scheduling user does not need such access simply to schedule concurrent programs.

- System Administrator
- Application Developer
- Acme GL Super User
- Acme AP Super User
- Acme PO Super User
- Acme AR Super User
- Cash Management
- Functional Administrator
- Alert Manager

Risk:

Application maintenance occurs through custom generic User

Recommendation:

Develop a custom Responsibility for job scheduling purposes only –
with access only to submit jobs and a limited set of concurrent
programs in the Request Group. Require use of login to be logged /
justified. Monitor its use via the Signon Audit Users report. See a
sample specification for this custom generic User at
www.erpra.net/books.html, follow the Book Resources link.

Level of Effort:

Medium

Priority:

High

Chapter 8: OV-6 Stale Users

Background:

The issue of stale users often doesn't have a lot of risk associated with it. I would consider it a secondary control that could identify issues with the de-provisioning (termination) process.

Risk:

Application maintenance (configurations, master data, or transactions) may occur by an unauthorized user of an account belonging to another user. This could be done by a person taking over the account and performing application maintenance using a login that doesn't belong to them. The taking over their account could be done by guessing their passwords, having access to their passwords, or through social engineering such as impersonating them to have the password reset.

Control Description:

Stale users are reviewed on a regular basis and disabled based on a policy adopted by the organization such as after 60 days without any activity.

Testing procedure:

Query 6: Stale Users

Comments related to testing:

This is a fairly simple query to evaluate. Some organizations user applications are assigned to all or a large number of users. Examples of such applications include: Employee Self-Service, iProcurement, and iExpense. In those cases, a significant number of stale users may exist and the organization may be reluctant to disable (end-date) the accounts. Therefore, it may be helpful to separate the results in two categories as part of the Observation:

- Those with access to only the low risk Responsibilities (such as Employee Self-Service)
- Those with access to other 'core' Responsibilities

If your time is limited, you may just want to provide the detail in an Appendix and let the client sort through which ones have high risk Responsibilities and which only have Responsibilities assigned with low risk.

Possible Finding language:

Following is potential language to document your finding:

Observation:

54 Users haven't logged into the applications in the last 60 days (i.e. are Stale Users). See detail below (or in an Appendix).

Risk:

Application maintenance (configurations, master data, or transactions) may occur by an unauthorized user of an account belonging to another user. This could be done by a person taking over the account and performing application maintenance using a login that doesn't belong to them. The taking over their account could be done by guessing their passwords, having access to their passwords, or through social engineering such as impersonating them to have the password reset.

Recommendation:

Develop a process for evaluating stale users on a regular basis (no less than monthly). Users with high risk access should be investigated as to why they haven't been used. If the account is stale because the employee has left the organization, evaluate the effectiveness of your termination process. If the employee is still at your organization, but not using the applications consider disabling the User account.

Level of Effort:

Medium

Priority:

High

Chapter 9: OV-7 Disabling accounts related to Terminated Users

Background:

Testing terminations is often heavily scrutinized. This query provides a quick way to see if any employees may have slipped through the cracks.

Risk:

Access for terminated employees, temporary workers, or contractors remain active allowing an unauthorized person to take over the account and perform application maintenance using a login that doesn't belong to them.

Control Description:

Access for employees, temporary workers, and contractors is disabled upon their termination from the organization.

Testing procedure:

Query 7: Possible Terminated Users

Comments related to testing:

This query returns a lot of data, but there are instructions in Chapter 36: Query 7: Possible Terminated Oracle Users that will help you filter through the data to get to the information that could be presented as an Observation. Admittedly this is a query I need to refine, but haven't had the time…

Possible Finding language:

Following is potential language to document your finding:

Observation:

Several employees have an HR termination date which have a Person Type of "Ex-Employee." See detail below (or in an Appendix).

Risk:

Access for terminated employees, temporary workers, or contractors remain active allowing an unauthorized person to take over the account and perform application maintenance using a login that doesn't belong to them.

Recommendation:

Review accounts to confirm whether any employees are no longer active. If these accounts relate to terminated employees (temporary employees or contractors) the User accounts should be end-dated.

If this is the case with one or more records, the termination procedures should be reviewed to determine how and why these user account(s) remain active after the employee is terminated

Level of Effort:

Medium

Priority:

High

Chapter 10: OV-8 AZN menus

Background:

AZN menus were introduced by Oracle around 11.5.5 (11i version – probably around 2005). If you find these used in one or more actively assigned Responsibilities, it could mean:

- If they went live prior to the menus being introduced, they were introduced as part of a patch and never identified as a risk to be removed
- If they went live after the AZN menus were introduced, it would indicate poor role design

More than likely, the organization doesn't know these menus exist and are accessible via various Responsibilities. There would be two findings associated with this observation.

Risk:

AZN menus inherently cause issues with excessive access to high risk functions, inappropriate access to sensitive data, and segregation of duties because they provide access to just about all the major transactions and master data elements related to a business process (like procure to pay or order to cash). Some AZN menus also provide access to high risk configurations within a business process.

When an AZN menu exists on a menu, the Processes tab as shown below becomes available:

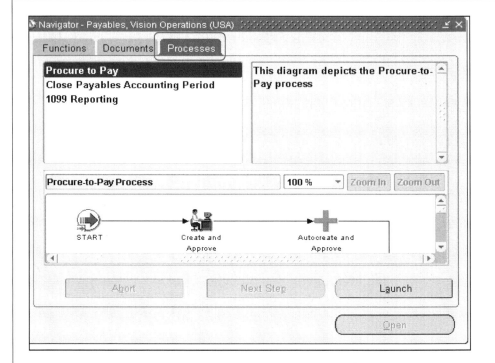

For more on this risk, see the YouTube video at:

https://www.youtube.com/watch?v=vdClsxHj9do which can be accessed at: www.YouTube.com/ERPRiskAdvisors.

Control Description:

AZN menus are not included in role design, unless specifically meant to be included and designed based on the principle of least privilege.

Testing procedure:

Query 3: Users with AZN menus

Comments related to testing:

Generally, if you find data returned from this query, you can use the results as a finding. However, there have been cases where the results of the query are a false positive. Therefore, I recommend you test a few of the records by validating in Query 1 that there is no Menu

Exclusion for the Responsibility. This will be explained further in the chapter below related to this Query 3.

Possible Finding language #1:

Following is potential language to document your finding:

Observation:

AZN Menus are accessible in 29 Responsibilities. See detail below (or in Appendix D).

Risk:

AZN menus have built-in SoD violations and may cause excessive access to high risk single functions. They should never be used to develop security.

See more on AZN menu risks at:

https://www.youtube.com/watch?v=vdClsxHj9do which can be accessed at: www.YouTube.com/ERPRiskAdvisors.

Recommendation:

AZN menus should not be assigned to anyone in Prod. They could be removed via a menu exclusion or a custom responsibility could be developed to give these users access to the related functions, but without access to the AZN menus.

Level of Effort:

Low

Priority:

High

Possible Finding language #2:

If you are confident the organization went live prior to version 11.5.5 (approximately 2005 or later – i.e. Release 10, 10.7, Release 11, or early versions of Release 11i), then this is a second finding:

Following is potential language to document your finding:

Observation:

Because AZN menus were introduced by Oracle via a patch, it appears the organization doesn't have a process to completely or accurately evaluate changes to application security introduced by patches.

Risk:

Users gaining access to Functions because of a patch that grants access to sensitive data, high risk Functions, or causes a Segregation of Duties violation.

Recommendation:

Organization needs to develop and implement a process to evaluate the impact of patches on their application security.

Level of Effort:

Medium

Priority:

High

Chapter 11: OV-9 Use of seeded Responsibilities

Background:

Generally, I don't recommend using any seeded Responsibilities, with few exceptions. An example of acceptable exceptions are those that have limited functionality such as iProcurement and iExpense. This chapter is focused on functional seeded Responsibilities. Later in the book, I will cover excessive access to IT functions.

Risk:

Seeded Responsibilities invariably have excessive access to high risk functions, inappropriate access to sensitive data, and segregation of duties because they often provide access to almost all the major transactions and master data elements related to a business process (i.e. procure to pay, order to cash). They also provide excessive access to configurations.

Control Description:

Responsibilities provided by Oracle are not assigned to Users unless every Function within that Responsibility is necessary to perform the work by those to whom the Responsibility is assigned. Samples include: Cash Management Superuser, General Ledger Super User, iSetup, Payables Manager, Project Billing Super User, Project Control (Full Access), Project Costing Super User, Project Super User. Purchasing Super User, Receivables Manager, Tax Managers, US HRMS Manager.

Testing procedure:

- Query 1: Responsibility Definitions
- Query 2: Users and Assigned Responsibilities

Comments related to testing:

This one is a bit more difficult to test unless you have knowledge of what is a seeded Responsibility (vs those that are custom). One way to test this is to use the list of seeded Responsibilities in the Control Description above.

Another way to address this is to first understand the naming conventions. Read more about this in Chapter 29: Query 1: Active Responsibility Definitions.

Possible Finding language:

Following is potential language to document your finding:

Observation:

Various employees have access to seeded "Super Users" Responsibilities. See detail below (or in an Appendix).

Risk:

Seeded Responsibilities invariably have excessive access to high risk functions, inappropriate access to sensitive data, and segregation of duties because they often provide access to almost all the major transactions and master data elements related to a business process (i.e. procure to pay, order to cash). They also provide excessive access to configurations.

Recommendation:

Seeded Responsibilities should not be assigned to anyone in Production, except in rare circumstances where the risk of such access is minimal (i.e. iProcurement, Workflow User).

Access for those supporting the applications should be built based on a risk-based approach to prevent SoD issues from being introduced to such Users. If such access is for IT users, we recommend a Support role and a Configuration role for each module.

The Support role for each module would have access to elements management deems necessary to support the applications. Ideally this is only inquiry access in Prod. However, there are some organizations where management believes sufficient mitigating controls exist for IT support users to have access to transactions and master data in Prod.

The Configuration role for each module would contain the forms and pages that management believes should be subject to the change management process. We don't recommend users having permanent access to the IT Configuration responsibilities unless there is a log- or trigger-based solution implemented to create a system based audit trail of changes and that system-based audit history is tested regularly for any unapproved changes. In cases where a log- or trigger-based auditing solution is not in place (and, therefore, there is no way to test for unapproved changes) we recommend the IT Configuration role only be assigned when a change ticket is approved and management has requested the change be made in Prod.

Level of Effort:

High

Priority:

High

Chapter 12: OV-10 Profile options risk assessment

Background:

If you are not familiar with Profile Options and the power they have to influence business process design and controls, take a look at the You Tube video "ERP Risk Advisors: Profile Options - What are they and Why Auditors Should Care" which can be accessed at our You Tube channel at: www.YouTube.com/ERPRiskAdvisors.

There are over 8,000 profile options in most environments. The majority of them are probably not relevant to the organization since they would relate to modules and functionality not being used by the organization.

Most organizations don't have a full appreciation for the risks associated with Profile Options. Therefore, they generally don't implement a process to effectively manage requests for changes. Often there isn't an understanding on who should evaluate or approve changes.

Also, often profile options are set during the original implementation based on minimal understanding and based on the 'expertise' of system integrators who typically are focused on operational effectiveness rather than control risk.

Because profile options can impact specific business processes, can be set at various levels, and, in some cases, shouldn't be set at all, or only set for a short period of time, documentation needs to be developed based on a risk assessment.

See an example risk assessment that can be used as a starting point at our website (www.erpra.net and the book resources page).

Risk:

The absence of a documented risk assessment process could allow for the setting of high risk profile options in Production. It could also cause profile options to be set at levels that are not appropriate such as a profile option being set at the User level or Responsibility level that would override a Site level setting; this may cause an override of controls.

Control Description:

A risk assessment has been performed that identifies which profile options can be set in the Production environment, at what level(s) they can be set, and who is authorized (if anyone) to approve the setting of or change to a profile option.

Testing procedure:

- Internal Controls Questionnaire
- Query 5: Profile Options

Comments related to testing:

If the response from the organization to the question posed in the ICQ is they have documented a profile options risk assessment, then you have evidence for the finding.

If they have a risk assessment documented, then you can review the results of Query 5 to identify one or more examples of profile options that are inappropriately set to provide evidence.

Possible Finding language:

Following is potential language to document your finding:

Observation:

There is no documentation provided to those who have access to profile option values to help them understand which profile options can be changed, at what levels (Site, Application, Responsibility, and User), and who can approve changes, if anyone.

Risk:

Various application settings can be maintained via profile options. Unauthorized or inappropriate changes to profile options could lead to changes in key control configurations, change in approvals processes, and/or changes in access to sensitive data. Some profile options could also allow for the corruption of data and performance issues. Examples include critical security parameters such as Utilities: Diagnostics and Utilities:SQL Trace.

Recommendation:

A risk assessment needs to be performed to evaluate and document the profile options that can be set in the application. Risk needs to be understood and an appropriate approver of profile option changes needs to be identified. In some cases, the approver can be the application administrator, in some cases the security group, and in some cases the profile option should be defaulted and never changed. ERP Risk Advisors has provided a template and starting point for this assessment which can be accessed at www.erpra.net/BookResources.html.

Start by documenting those that are in the risk assessment template provided by ERP Risk Advisors, evaluate those set in your organization, and add to the risk assessment as changes are requested.

Level of Effort:

Medium

Priority:

High

Chapter 13: OV-11 High risk profile options

Background:

This chapter compliments the prior chapter with a focus on improperly set profile options. If the organization has documented a risk assessment use that as a starting point. However, even in that case you should use our risk assessment (refer to www.erpra.net on the book resources page) as our risk assessment template may have some profile options that should also be evaluated.

If the organization hasn't documented a risk assessment, then use our risk assessment to determine whether the high risk profile options are appropriately set.

Risk:

Inappropriate or unapproved setting of high risk profile options. This could lead to many issues; for example, unapproved back door access to the database, performance issues, excessive data growth, unnecessary exposure of applications to the internet, and configurations not consistent with control design.

There are over 8,000 profile options in most environments. Your organization should have a full understanding of risks documented as part of the profile options risk assessment.

Control Description:

Profile options are set and approved based on a risk assessment performed by the organization.

Testing procedure:

Query 5: Profile Options

Comments related to testing:

Check for regular updates to the Profile Option Risk Assessment on the Book Resources page at www.erpra.net/Books.html. Use Query 5 and the sample profile options risk assessment to review those deemed high risk in the profile options risk assessment. Document those that are different from the recommendations in the risk assessment template or that you believe undermine controls in the organization.

Possible Finding language:

Following is potential language to document your finding:

Observation:

Certain profile options have not been set appropriately.

Examples include:

- Journals: Allow Preparer Approval – is set to Yes at the Site level
- Utilities:Diagnostics – is set to Yes at the Site level and should not be allowed at any level in Prod.

User overrides have been set when not appropriate.

- Signon Password No Reuse – which is set to 9999 for the User "SYSADMIN"

Some profile options that should be set have not been set at all.

- GLDI: Journal Source is not set at any level

Risk:

Inappropriate or unapproved setting of high risk profile options. This could lead to many issues; for example, unapproved back door access to the database, performance issues, excessive data growth, unnecessary exposure of applications to the internet, and configurations not consistent with control design.

There are over 8,000 profile options in most environments. Your organization should have a full understanding of risks documented as part of the profile options risk assessment.

Recommendation:

The setting of profile options needs to be review for every application. Those that are set need to be reviewed to make sure they are appropriate and consistent with the Profile Options Risk Assessment performed by the organization.

Examples are:

- Personalize Self-Service Defn
- Utilities:Diagnostics
- FND: Debug Log Enabled

In some cases certain profile options should be set, but are not. Examples are:

- Signon Password No Reuse
- Sign-On:Audit Level
- GLDI: Journal Source

Both of these should be set in Production:

- Signon Password No Reuse should be set according to policy. If there is no policy, one should be developed.
- Sign-On:Audit Level should at least be set to User to track user logins to be able to monitor logins for generic logins such as SYSADMIN which should be logged per the comments above related to generic users

Level of Effort:

High

Priority:

High

Chapter 14: OV-12 User profile values

Background:

Oracle provides a form allowing users to set certain profile options. Following is screen shot of this form:

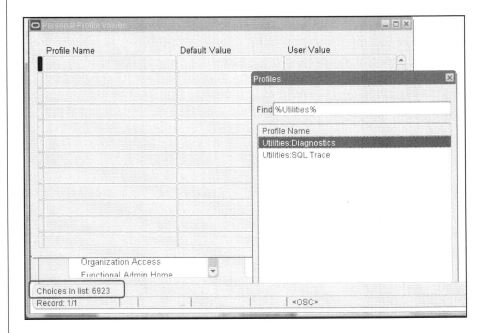

With this form, allows a profile option can be set at the User level, overriding other values such as those set at the Site, Application, or Responsibility level. Whether a profile option can be set through this form is defined in the Profile Options form. You can see the number of choices in the list is 6923. This means that 6923 different profile options can either be viewed or updated through this form.

An example of this form follows – the User Access box identifies whether or not it can be updated through the Personal Profile Values form:

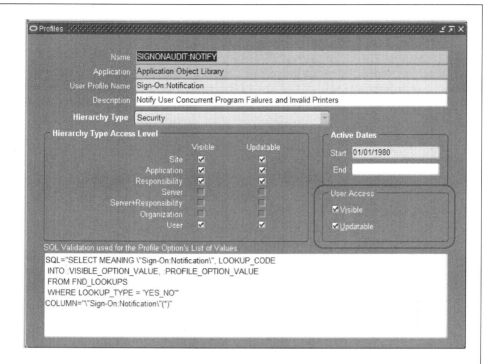

Risk:

This form allows users to set profile options at the User level for thousands of profile options. This would allow them to override profile options set at the Site, Application, and Responsibility levels.

See more on this risk at:
https://www.youtube.com/watch?v=2wK4Mj_-XgM which can be accessed at: www.YouTube.com/ERPRiskAdvisors.

Control Description:

Access to the Personal Profile Values form has been removed or the form has been personalized to restrict its use to profile options that have low risk and management believes Users should maintain.

Testing procedure:

Query 12: High Risk Single Functions as follows:

Comments related to testing:

Query 12 includes the Functions (Define User Profile Options (FNDPOMPO), Profile User Values (FND_FNDPOMSV)) that relate to the User Profile Values form (as known as Personal Profile Values). The User Profile Values is often found in EVERY Responsibility unless it is specifically excluded since it is included in the same menu used to run concurrent programs (Requests: Submit). Therefore, I often find it available for some Responsibilities even if it has been excluded from others.

Keep in mind that Query 12 does NOT take into account Function exclusions or Menu exclusions. If the organization you are auditing has attempted to restrict access to this form by using Function exclusions at the Responsibility level, you will also need to review the data in Query 1: Responsibilities to confirm whether or not these Functions have been excluded from the Responsibility. You should be able to provide a few examples. You shouldn't need to provide a complete list in order to have an effective finding.

Possible Finding language:

Following is potential language to document your finding:

Observation:

Several Responsibilities still have the ability to override profile options via the Personal Profile Values form – see detail below (or Appendix).

Risk:

This form allows users to set profile options at the User level for thousands of profile options. This would allow them to override profile options set at the Site, Application, and Responsibility levels.

See more on this risk at:
https://www.youtube.com/watch?v=2wK4Mj_-XgM which can be at: www.YouTube.com/ERPRiskAdvisors.

Recommendation:

Remove access to User Profile Values form for all users in Prod.

Alternatively, the form could be personalized to only provide the ability to set the values for low risk Profile Options that would be identified as part of a risk assessment process.

Level of Effort:

Medium

Priority:

High

Chapter 15: OV-13 System profile values

Background:

The System Profile Values form is the form where profile options are typically set. Following is an example:

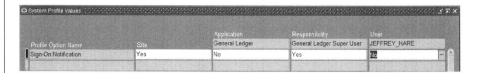

Profile Option Name	Site	Application General Ledger	Responsibility General Ledger Super User	User JEFFREY_HARE
Sign-On:Notification	Yes	No	Yes	No

This is the same profile option shown in the prior chapter which can be set through the User Profile Options form. Note that it can also be set at the User level here in addition to being able to be set at the Site, Application, and Responsibility level as shown above.

Following again is the configuration of this Profile Option with the levels it can be set identified in the "Hierarchy Type Access Level box:

```
Name       SIGNONAUDIT:NOTIFY
Application Application Object Library
User Profile Name  Sign-On:Notification
Description Notify User Concurrent Program Failures and Invalid Printers
Hierarchy Type  Security
```

Hierarchy Type Access Level

	Visible	Updatable
Site	☑	☑
Application	☑	☑
Responsibility	☑	☑
Server	☐	☐
Server+Responsibility	☐	☐
Organization	☐	☐
User	☑	☑

Active Dates
Start 01/01/1980
End

User Access
☑ Visible
☑ Updatable

SQL Validation used for the Profile Option's List of Values

```
SQL="SELECT MEANING \"Sign-On:Notification\", LOOKUP_CODE
INTO :VISIBLE_OPTION_VALUE, :PROFILE_OPTION_VALUE
FROM FND_LOOKUPS
WHERE LOOKUP_TYPE = 'YES_NO'"
COLUMN="\"Sign-On:Notification\"(*)"
```

Risk:

Access to the System Profile Values form allows a User to set and make changes to profile options at all levels. The risk is inappropriate setting or changes to profile options leading to issues such as unapproved back door access to the database, performance issues, excessive data growth, and configurations not consistent with control design. Those with access to this form in Prod should have a full understanding of risks documented as part of the profile options risk assessment.

Having this form accessible by more than just a couple of Users dilutes the quality of the evaluation of request for change and could lead to inappropriate or unapproved changes to Profile Options.

Control Description:

Access to the System Profile Values form has been restricted to only those users authorized to make changes to profile options. Users provided access to this form follow the guidelines in the Profile Option Risk assessment as documented by management.

Testing procedure:

Query 12: High Risk Single Functions

Comments related to testing:

Query 12 includes the Functions (Profile System Values (FND_FNDPOMPV)) that relate to the System Profile Values form. Keep in mind that Query 12 does NOT take into account Function exclusions or Menu exclusions. If the organization you are auditing has attempted to restrict access to this form by using Function exclusions and Menu exclusions at the Responsibility level, you will also need to review the data in Query 1: Responsibilities to confirm whether or not these Functions have been excluded from the Responsibility.

Possible Finding language:

Following is potential language to document your finding:

Observation:

System Profile Values for is accessible by 42 Users through 10 Responsibilities

Risk:

Access to the System Profile Values form allows a User to set and make changes to profile options at all levels. The risk is inappropriate setting or changes to profile options leading to issues such as unapproved back door access to the database, performance issues, excessive data growth, and configurations not consistent with control design. Those with access to this form in Prod should have a full understanding of risks documented as part of the profile options risk assessment.

Having this form accessible by more than just a couple of Users dilutes the quality of the evaluation of request for change and could lead to inappropriate or unapproved changes to Profile Options.

Recommendation:

We typically recommend limiting access to just a few employees (only two, if possible, based on the volume of changes) in most organizations. Those with access to this form should be trained in the change management process and have access to the Profile Options Risk Assessment performed by the organization.

Level of Effort:

Low

Priority:

High

Chapter 16: OV-14 Access to high risk concurrent programs

Background:

Concurrent Programs are background jobs that could either be a report or it could process data. I often find that many organizations have paid little attention to designing access to Concurrent Programs. Concurrent Programs can be accessed through either the Request Group which is associated with a Responsibility or through a Function assigned to a Menu.

I am not covering Concurrent Programs that can be accessed via a Function at this time. There are 792 Functions as of the writing of this book. I will probably address this in the next version of the book.

This chapter covers Concurrent Programs that are covered through Request Group access. Each Responsibility can be defined with a Request Group, but a Request Group is not required.

Following is a screen shot of the Responsibility form where you can see where a Request Group is defined:

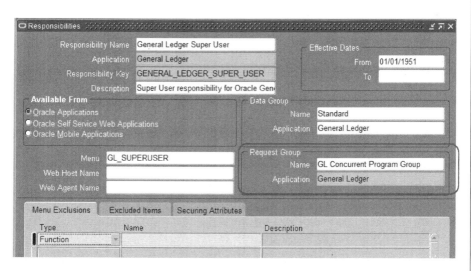

There is more on this subject in the SQL queries 10a – 10d.

Risk:

Excessive access to high risk concurrent programs (such as interface, processing, archive, and purge programs) and inappropriate access to sensitive data.

Control Description:

Request groups are designed based on the principle of least privilege. Each Responsibility is developed with a custom request group with only those programs and reports that are necessary for the Role for which the Responsibility is designed.

Testing procedure:

- 10a What request groups have access to what programs
- 10b Request sets contained in Request Groups
- 10c "Application" type entries in Request Groups
- 10d Definition of Request Sets

Comments related to testing:

Similar to role design covered in Chapter 5: OV-3 Role design, this is another one of those topics that could take several chapters. The essence of this test is to identify whether or not users have access to concurrent programs that are not appropriate for their role. There are some concurrent programs I recommend that NO users have in Prod or only have access in Prod for a temporary basis as part of a change cycle.

Giving you the definitive list of 'high risk' concurrent programs is impossible. I have provided you a list in the Book Resources page on our website. However, this list should not be considered to be comprehensive. I recommend you develop your own list based on the programs your users have access to currently in Prod. I will update the template as I identify those that should be considered high risk. I would also appreciate you sending me any that you believe should be added to the list so I can update the list. Let's collaborate to continue developing this list. The file can be accessed from a link at: erpra.net/books.html.

Possible Finding language #1:

Following is potential language to document your finding:

Observation:

We identified various concurrent programs that are inappropriate assigned to users in Prod. Appendix A has detailed examples.

Risk:

Access to certain programs such as those that allow purging, archiving, and decryption of data is inappropriate in Prod and could lead to corruption of your environment or exposure of sensitive data. Additionally other programs are inappropriate for the roles they are assigned. Inquiry Responsibilities should not have access to any concurrent programs that process data. These issues could lead to unauthorized users running concurrent programs that process data and unauthorized access to sensitive data.

Recommendation:

Each custom role should have a custom Request Group with access to only the concurrent programs and reports that are relevant for that role. We typically don't recommend assignment of concurrent programs via functions since those functions reference request groups that are routinely updated by Oracle through patches. Therefore, any and all concurrent programs that are needed for a role are built into a custom Request Group specifically designed for that Responsibility.

Level of Effort:

High

Priority:

High

Possible Finding language #2:

Observation:

Organization does not have a mature and complete process for identifying, classifying and protecting sensitive data.

There is no list of sensitive data that identifies the process owner, what objects (functions and request groups) have access to such data, what tables and views that can access such data.

Based on discussions, we don't believe organization has identified specific users at the application and database level that can access sensitive data.

Risk:

Inappropriate or unapproved access or changes to sensitive data.

Recommendation:

Organization needs to initiate and complete a sensitive data project that:

- Identifies sensitive data elements and data owner for each element
- Identifies tables where sensitive data is stored
- Identifies objects that have access to sensitive data
- Reviews access to sensitive data via functions and request groups
- Reviews access to database through database logins – custom and seeded

Level of Effort:

High

Priority:

High

Possible Finding language #3:

Observation:

There is no list of sensitive / high risk concurrent programs (standard and custom). This has led to excessive access to high risk reports such as those identified in Appendix A.

Risk:

Inappropriate processing or purging of data by Users that are unauthorized to do so.

Recommendation:

Sensitive concurrent program listing needs to be developed with an approver for each so that security administrators that manage Request Groups

Level of Effort:

High

Priority:

High

Chapter 17: OV-15 Chart of accounts maintenance

Background:

Access to change the chart of accounts is done through three Functions that all related to the same Form. The risks related to access in this form go beyond just access to the Chart of Accounts. However, these same Functions are used to maintain value sets throughout the application. This is a shared form where anyone with access to it can maintain ANY value set.

Risk:

The risk is unapproved changes are made to chart of accounts values. This could lead to values being posted to wrong accounts or not being reported on financial statements.

Control Description:

Access to maintain the value sets related to the chart of accounts is restricted to the employees that are authorized to make such changes. Because the form through which this data is maintained is often used in modules other than the General Ledger, the risks are that those are authorized make changes to the value sets related to the chart of accounts. Management has evaluated the risk and implemented one of these four options:

1. Allow access to Users outside accounting and monitor the changes to make sure all additions and changes to the Chart of Accounts are appropriate and authorized

2. Personalize the form to restrict who can maintain which value sets

3. Accept the risk

4. In release 12.2 and later, value set security can be implemented through the User Management module (see Flexfields Guide, Release 12.2, Part No. E22963-08 for more information)

Testing procedure:

Query 12: High Risk Single Functions

Comments related to testing:

There are three functions that give a user the ability to maintain the chart of accounts values. Note that this is the SAME form that is used to maintain values in value sets used by other modules, by descriptive flexfields, and could be used to develop a list of values for custom development. In other words, this form is used to create values in a LOT of place in the applications. Therefore, it is typically accessible by many users. Many of the users that have access to the form would NOT be authorized to make changes to the chart of accounts – hence the need to monitor who is making changes to which values or to 'break apart' this form either through developed (prior to 12.2) or via Flexfield Security introduced in R12.2. The three functions are:

User Function Name	Function Name
Descriptive Flexfield Values	FND_FNDFFMSV_DESCR
Flexfield Values	FND_FNDFFMSV
Key Flexfield Values	FND_FNDFFMSV_KEY

These three functions all point to the same underlying form "Segment Values". The only difference is the 'focus' of the Find form, the button is defaulted differently for each of the Functions (Value Set, Key Flexfield, or Descriptive Flexfield – see below).

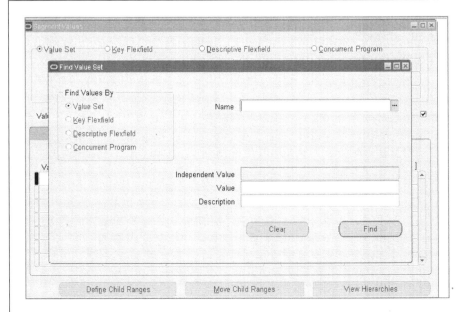

In reality, the risks related to this form is not just "unapproved changes are made to chart of accounts values", but unapproved changes to any value set used throughout the instance. I highlight the risk as related to the chart of accounts, but it is the best way to get the attention of executives related to the shared use of this form. If you tell the CFO or Controller that Users outside the accounting department can maintain or add values to the chart of accounts, usually it rises to the top of the list faster than if you tell a purchasing manager that someone in accounting can maintain their data.

Possible Finding language:

Following is potential language to document your finding:

Observation:

There appears to be excessive access to maintain Flexfield values through the following functions:

User Function Name	Function Name
Descriptive Flexfield Values	FND_FNDFFMSV_DESCR
Flexfield Values	FND_FNDFFMSV
Key Flexfield Values	FND_FNDFFMSV_KEY

Details can be found in Appendix A.

Risk:

Since this form can access ANY values set, any user with access to this form can maintain any add values to ANY value set. Commonly, the most significant risk is unapproved changes being made to chart of accounts values by users outside the accounting department. This could lead to values being posted to wrong accounts or not being reported on financial statements. However, this form maintains values for all key flexfields throughout the suite, they are typically used in descriptive flexfields, and also in custom development. Therefore, there are risks of unapproved changes throughout the applications where value sets are used.

Recommendation:

To offset this risk, four options are available:

1. Allow access to other users and monitor the changes to make sure any changes to the Chart of Accounts are appropriate and authorized

2. Personalize the form to restrict who can maintain which value sets

3. Accept the risk

4. In release 12.2 and later, value set security can be implemented through the User Management module

Level of Effort:

Medium

Priority:

High

Chapter 18: OV-16 Password policy - expiration date

Background:

The password expiration days for Users are not set on an overall basis like through a profile option, but rather are set for each user individually through the Users form. Following is an example:

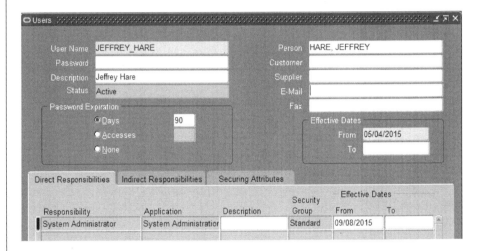

Password Expiration is set to '90', but has to be set manually when a User is created.

Risk:

Risks are as follows:

1. Non-compliance with the policy.

2. Someone other than the owner of the User account takes over the account, usually through the re-setting of the password, in order to perform activities to which they are not authorized.

Control Description:

Passwords related to User accounts are set up to expire according to the organization's policy at such time the user must change the password the next time they log in.

Testing procedure:

Query 11: Users outside of Password Expiration Policy

Comments related to testing:

This one is easy to test as long as the correct policy is entered in the SQL query. Most often we find that generic users don't have the password expiration days set. There is a misconception that if the password expires the account becomes disabled or locked. This is not the case. When password expires, it means the next time that account is used to log in, the system requires the user to change the password. Those that 'own' generic accounts should log in at the necessary interval (90 days if that is your policy) to change the password just like any other user account.

Possible Finding language:

Following is potential language to document your finding:

Observation:

Users in Appendix A were noted to NOT have a User Password Expiration Days or have their Password Expiration days with a value other than the policy set by the organization.

Risk:

- Non-compliance with policy
- Someone other than the owner of the User account takes over the account, usually through hacking or decrypting of the password, in order to perform activities to which they are not authorized.

NOTE: The risk could be partially mitigated if the profile option "Signon Password Failure Limit" is set to '3' (IF YOU HAVE CONFIRMED THIS FROM QUERY 5)

Recommendation:

All users, even GUEST should have their password expire every 90 (or whatever the policy states) days according the policy adopted by your organization. Exceptions, to the extent allowed, should be documented in the policy or a standards document.

Level of Effort:

Low

Priority:

High

Chapter 19: OV-17 Password policy compliance

Background:

This chapter covers the rest of password-related configurations that are set through profile options. Note that all of these profile options can be set at the Site level (which would apply globally to all users) and at the User level, which would override the Site level setting. This setting at the User level would have to be done through the System Profile Values form (with the exception of Sign-On:Notification which could be set through either the System Profile Values form or the User Profile Values form).

Risk:

Risks are as follows:

- Non-compliance with the policy.
- Someone other than the owner of the User account takes over the account, usually through hacking or decrypting of the password, in order to perform activities to which they are not authorized.

Control Description:

The following profile options are set to support the organization's policies:

- Signon Password Case
- Signon Password Failure Limit
- Signon Password Hard to Guess
- Signon Password Length
- Signon Password No Reuse
- Signon Password Custom
- Sign-On:Notification

Testing procedure:

Query 5: Profile Options

Comments related to testing:

This is fairly easy to test using query 5. Keep in mind that several of these can be set at the User level or a level other than the Site level which is where you would expect it to be set. Therefore, when reviewing the results of query 5, make sure you look for this being set at any level.

Note, for organizations that have implemented a single sign-on / identity management solution, some accounts can still be logged in directly through a local URL. This is necessary for job scheduling accounts and seeded accounts like SYSADMIN. Therefore, these profile options should be set even if those cases.

Possible Finding language:

Following is potential language to document your finding:

Observation:

One or more of the profile options related to password controls is not set consistently with the organization's policy. See detail below (or in Appendix ...)

Risk:

Risks are as follows:

- Non-compliance with the policy.
- Someone other than the owner of the User account takes over the account, usually through hacking or decrypting of the password, in order to perform activities to which they are not authorized.

Recommendation:

These profile options should be set according to policy. Any exceptions to this policy that are approved by management should be documented in the policy or a standards document referenced by the policy.

Level of Effort:

Low

Priority:

High

Chapter 20: OV-18 Access to sensitive administrative pages and forms

Background:

This is undoubtedly the most important topic in this book. I often see this issue being entirely unaddressed by organizations and yet it is one of the most significant security risks in the applications. See more on this topic in Oracle's MOS Note 403537.1. I am shocked at how many organizations I talk to that are not aware of MOS Note 403537.1 which is called "Secure Configuration Guide for Oracle E-Business Suite Release 12."

See also video on this topic at: www.youtube.com/watch?v=p73NqKU3ppA which can be accessed at: www.youtube.com/user/ERPRiskAdvisors.

Risk:

Unauthorized or inappropriate execution of an ad hoc SQL statements. In some cases, the form support the execution of an Operating System script. These forms basically allow any user to change any data in the system similar to what a DBA could do using the 'APPS' password. These forms have complete, unrestricted ability to execute a DML statement (Insert, Update, and Delete) and a DDL statement (such as TRUNC, DROP, and ALTER). The forms that allow Operating System scripts to be executed can run any OS script – one example being a script to reset any password – such as SYSADMIN or another user that has access to the System Administrator responsibility. Malicious use of these forms / pages could allow a user to change any data, such as the changing of a supplier's bank account. The use of these forms / page could also lead to resetting other User accounts and doing any maintenance through another account. It could also lead to corruption of the database through changing internal ID's or deleting or altering tables.

Control Description:

Access to forms and pages that allow SQL injection and OS scripts to be run through them are restricted to Users that are authorized to use them. Management has reviewed and accepted the risk of such access. Additionally, management has appropriately evaluated options for monitoring activity through these forms such as the use of a trigger-based or log-based monitoring solution. Management has either implemented a trigger-based or log-based monitoring solution or has documented acceptance of the risks noted above.

Testing procedure:

Query 12: High Risk Single Functions

Internal Controls Questionnaire – Question #1

Comments related to testing:

Testing this through query 12 is better than nothing, but can be problematic given the fact that it doesn't take into account Menu or Function Exclusions. This often results in lots of false positives because several of the functions in these queries are contained in setup menus that are commonly excluded via Menu Exclusions.

My favorite solution to implement to monitor activity in these 60 or so Functions is CS*Audit from CaoSys. We are a key partner with CaoSys and have built content for CS*Audit that make monitoring the underlying tables easy to do.

On this topic, I usually present two findings. The first relates to excessive access to these forms and page. I take the results in Query 12 and present them 'as is' with the caveat that some of the results could be false positives since the function could be excluded via a Menu or Function Exclusion in the Responsibilities form.

The second finding relates to the absence of a trigger-based or log-based solution to monitor the activity through these forms. It is impossible to remove access to all these forms because many are used by functional and IT users on a regular basis.

Possible Finding language 1:

Following is potential language to document your finding:

Observation:

There are 37 users that have access to forms and pages that allow SQL injection in Prod. See detail in Appendix I.

Risk:

Unauthorized or inappropriate execution of an ad hoc SQL statements. In some cases, the form support the execution of an Operating System script. These forms basically allow any user to change any data in the system similar to what a DBA could do using the 'APPS' password. These forms have complete, unrestricted ability to execute a DML statement (Insert, Update, and Delete) and a DDL statement (such as TRUNC, DROP, and ALTER). The forms that allow Operating System scripts to be executed can run any OS script – one example being a script to reset any password – such as SYSADMIN or another user that has access to the System Administrator responsibility. Malicious use of these forms / pages could allow a user to change any data, such as the changing of a supplier's bank account. The use of these forms / page could also lead to resetting other User accounts and doing any maintenance through another account. It could also lead to corruption of the database through changing internal ID's or deleting or altering tables.

Recommendation:

Access to these forms needs to be VERY tightly controlled so that your risk is contained to as few Users as possible.

For those that do have access a policy needs to be developed that all activity through these forms are subject to the change management process, including a peer review of the activity.

A trigger or log-based solution needs to be put in place to monitor the activity at the database level. We recommend implementing such a solution for the tables for all 63 Functions that allow SQL injection or OS execution, not just the Functions that are assigned in your environment. This would take into account a User getting access to one or more of the forms that aren't currently accessible in Prod.

Finally, a group independent of those that have access to the forms / page audits the actual changes from the trigger- or log-based audit trail to look for unapproved changes. This includes tracing 100% of all activity back to the approved activity.

Level of Effort:

High

Priority:

High

Possible Finding language 2:

If the organization does not have a trigger- or log-based solution to build the detailed audit trail, this is a possible second solution…

Following is potential language to document your finding:

Observation:

Organization does not monitor activity in the forms that allow SQL injection and Operating Script to be executed from within them. There are over 60 known forms. See more on this topic in Oracle's MOS Note 403537.1. See also video on this topic at: www.youtube.com/watch?v=p73NqKU3ppA which can be accessed at: www.youtube.com/user/ERPRiskAdvisors.

See Appendix H for two examples of how these forms can be used to commit fraud. (See Book Resources page at www.erpra.net for the examples to include in the report if you wish).

(If you wanted a more targeted risk you could use this one):

Organization does not have technology deployed that audits changes to the vendor master. Current controls would not catch someone setting up a fictitious vendor either through current access to a VENDOR MASTER role, an unsecured database login, or a form that allows SQL injection. The greatest risk would the switching of a bank account on a high dollar existing supplier that is being paid via ACH. The only way this fraud would be detected given current controls is when the vendor would call asking why they weren't paid. Even in that scenario it may be difficult to determine who made the change to the vendor because of the ability to use SQL form injection, execute an Operating System script, or through a database login in Prod with update access to these tables.

Risk:

Unauthorized or inappropriate execution of an ad hoc SQL statements. In some cases, the form support the execution of an Operating System script. These forms basically allow any user to change any data in the system similar to what a DBA could do using the 'APPS' password. These forms have complete, unrestricted ability to execute a DML statement (Insert, Update, and Delete) and a DDL statement (such as TRUNC, DROP, and ALTER). The forms that allow Operating System scripts to be executed can run any OS script – one example being a script to reset any password – such as SYSADMIN or another user that has access to the System Administrator responsibility. Malicious use of these forms / pages could allow a user to commit fraud such as the changing of a supplier's bank account.

Recommendation:

A trigger- or log-based auditing solution should be put in place that audits key changes to data throughout the application. Organization needs to identify the tables that need to be monitored based on an overall risk assessment that takes into account activity in the following categories:

- Configurations, especially those subject to change control and those that support Application Controls
- Development objects
- Security objects
- Object that are core to the application such as Key Flexfields, Descriptive Flexfields, Value Sets, Ledger Setup, Organizations, etc.
- Master data such as Customer Master, Item Master, Supplier Master, and Flexfield Values
- Forms / pages that accept SQL statements and can run OS scripts

Level of Effort:

High

Priority:

Critical

Chapter 21: OV-19 Excessive access to Alert Manager

Background:

Alert Manager contains one of the forms that allow for the execution of ad hoc SQL statements and OS scripts. It one of the forms that is easy to understand how it can be used. Therefore, it is a good example to bring forth to highlight that risk. I find that there are often many users that have access to this in Prod. This Responsibility has two purposes: 1. To create or maintain the Alerts; 2. To schedule the Alerts to monitor activity in Prod.

Commonly the development staff who develop Alerts are given access to set up and schedule the Alerts in Prod. As part of the testing of this control, you review the list of IT Users as provided in response to the ICQ and see if any developers have access to this in Prod. If you do, it opens up the discussion of why. Commonly accepted best practices would segregate the development work from the migration of such work to Prod. Usually a developer 'develops' the work then someone independent of the development team (could be an operations team or the DBAs) moves the development to a test environment for user acceptance testing for testing. Then the same group / person moves the development to Prod.

This protocol – Dev / Test / Prod where developers only have access to a Dev environment is nearly ALWAYS used for object-oriented development, yet we it is not being the case for 'development' that is done through form (such as Alerts, but also including Configuration changes). Therefore, if developers have access to Alert Manager, it opens the discussion of why. Why are developers allowed to make changes in Prod for Alerts when this isn't following industry best practices and isn't consistent with how the organization is handling object-oriented development.

Risk:

Unauthorized or inappropriate execution of an ad hoc SQL statements. In some cases, the form support the execution of an Operating System script. These forms basically allow any user to change any data in the system similar to what a DBA could do using the 'APPS' password. These forms have complete, unrestricted ability to execute a DML statement (Insert, Update, and Delete) and a DDL statement (such as TRUNC, DROP, and ALTER). The forms that allow Operating System scripts to be executed can run any OS script – one example being a script to reset any password – such as SYSADMIN or another user that has access to the System Administrator responsibility. Malicious use of these forms / pages could allow a user to commit fraud such as the changing of a supplier's bank account.

Control Description:

Access to the Alert Manager responsibility is tightly restricted (ideally no more than two people) because of its ability to allow an ad hoc SQL statement and an Operating System script to be executed from it. Management has reviewed and accepted the risk of such access.

Testing procedure:

Query 2: Users and Assigned Responsibilities

Comments related to Testing:

This finding is similar to the finding in OV-18 above. I suggest calling this out as a specific finding because it is the one form that is easiest to understand and most commonly is assigned to a large number of IT users. The Alert Manager Responsibility contains one of the forms used in the examples in my YouTube video on SQL injections which can be accessed at: www.youtube.com/user/ERPRiskAdvisors.

Identify how many users have access to Alert Manager through Query 2. Often I see four or five or more users having access in Prod. The question you need to pose is how many of those that have access are actually authorized to make changes in Prod. Ask about the roles of those that have access. If they are developers, ask why developers have access to Prod. Ask why someone independent of the development of these isn't moving the Alerts from the Development environment to a Test environment for user acceptance testing and why that same person or group isn't moving the change to Prod. This protocol should be the same protocol as would be used for an object change that would go through the change management process. Why would the same protocol not be used for Alerts?

I also see the full Alert Manager responsibility being assigned to one or more generic users such as SYSADMIN and a job scheduling users. Such generic logins are typically shared logins. This leaves the organization with no accountable related to changes in the case where the Alert Manager responsibility is used to run a SQL script or an operating script.

In lieu of having the full Alert Manager responsibility, just the form that is used to schedule Alerts could be assigned to the job scheduling user- developed in a custom responsibility or added to an existing custom responsibility. See www.erpra.net/books.html for a link to the resources where a specification is provided for a job scheduling user and related responsibility.

Possible Finding language:

Following is potential language to document your finding:

Observation:

Six users have access to Alert Manager. See detail in Appendix B.

Risk:

Unauthorized or inappropriate execution of an ad hoc SQL statements. In some cases, the form support the execution of an Operating System script. These forms basically allow any user to change any data in the system similar to what a DBA could do using the 'APPS' password. These forms have complete, unrestricted ability to execute a DML statement (Insert, Update, and Delete) and a DDL statement (such as TRUNC, DROP, and ALTER). The forms that allow Operating System scripts to be executed can run any OS script – one example being a script to reset any password – such as SYSADMIN or another user that has access to the System Administrator responsibility. Malicious use of these forms / pages could allow a user to commit fraud such as the changing of a supplier's bank account.

Recommendation:

Access to these forms needs to be VERY tightly controlled so that your risk is contained to as few Users as possible.

For those that do have access a policy needs to be developed that all activity through these forms are subject to the change management process.

Then, a trigger or log-based solution needs to be put in place to monitor the activity at the database level. We actually recommend implementing such a solution for the tables for all 63 Functions that allow SQL injection or OS execution

Finally, a group independent of those that have access audits the actual changes from the trigger- or log-based audit trail to look for unapproved changes.

Level of Effort:

High

Priority:

Critical

Chapter 22: OV-20 Excessive access to IT functions

Background:

I often find some of the worst role design comes in the IT department. Most IT organizations do a great job designing policies and procedures when it comes to object-oriented development. However, when it comes to other activities in the IT department, fall short. Too often I find seeded Responsibilities assigned to Users even though seeded Responsibilities have excessive access to high risk Functions and don't reflect proper change management practices.

This chapter focuses on the basics. IT access should be based on the principle of least privilege. IT users should have access to the functions they need to do their job, no more... no less. This means a Security Administrator doesn't need Functions that should only be assigned to a DBA as is the case when they are assigned the Security Administrator Responsibility. A developer shouldn't have access in Prod at all since it violates basic Segregation of Duties principles segregating development from migration to Production. Yet, developers are often given access to Alert Manager, Functional Administrator or Functional Developer.

The start of good role design in the IT department is custom roles for each of the groups that are authorized to have access in Prod.

Risk:

Excessive access to IT functions that related to user provisioning, system administration, profile options, security objects (such as Menus, Request Groups, and Responsibilities), development objects (Functions, Forms, Executables, Concurrent Programs), and other high risk IT functionality. This could lead to the following:

- Inappropriate or unapproved changes to data including security and development data as a result of lack of training or oversight
- Segregation of duties violations – for example: development objects are registered in Production by the same person doing the development – see IIA GTAG 2 which suggests that development objects should not be migrated to Prod via the development group. Implied is that these objects should be registered by someone other than the development group to maintain this SoD. Of greater risk is that developer access to Prod could change the

definition of one or more development objects to change the functionality that could be achieved via that object.

- Currently none of the security or development objects are being audited via a trigger-based auditing solution so no quality assurance process is yet implemented. Therefore, unapproved changes could be happening in Prod with no process to detect them.
- Lack of peer review for development changes

Control Description:

IT access to the applications is developed based on the principle of least privilege by designing custom roles for IT users such as DBAs, developers, security administrators, and business analysts. Usually this means the following seeded Responsibilities are NOT assigned in Production: (Application Developer, Functional Administrator, Functional Developer, System Administration. System Administrator, User Management, SFM System Administrator) since they contain functions that are not appropriate for any one single role. As such, custom Responsibilities are developed for each of the roles within the IT organization. As Responsibilities are developed for each of the custom roles, a 'Support' responsibility and a 'Configuration' Responsibility is normally needed. The Support responsibility would be something would be something the employee would have in Production at all times. The Configuration responsibility would be something that typically only be assigned when a change ticket has been approved or in conjunction with a release into Production.

Testing procedure:

Query 2: Users and Assigned Responsibilities

Comments related to testing:

Typically all is needed to test this to identify a finding is to review query 2 which identifies the active Users and their assigned Responsibilities. Typically I find a lot of IT users having access to these Responsibilities in Prod: Application Developer, Functional Administrator, Functional Developer, System Administration, System Administrator, User Management, and SFM System Administrator.

For those that have access to these Responsibilities in Prod it may be necessary to identify the role these employees serve in the organization. Following are a couple of examples you can probe further, if necessary.

Scenario 1: Security administrator access to DBA functions. A security administrator has access to the System Administrator responsibility which has access to the menu related to System Administration menu. Functions under the System Administration menu typically are restricted to the DBAs if they are accessible to anyone in Prod.

Scenario 2: Developer access to Prod Functions. Typically developers should not have any access to Prod. Allowing developers access to Prod typically causes a violation to the Segregation of Duties between developers and those that move changes to Prod. Most organizations understand this concept and hold to it strictly related to 'development' objects such as packages, stored procedures, forms, web pages, etc. However, when it comes to changes that are done through forms or pages, the standards go out the window. Therefore, finding development staff that have any access to Prod is typically a sign that access to IT functions have not been properly developed.

Simply ask the question – why is it developers can't move objects to Prod, but they can make changes to the forms or pages to Prod?

Scenario 3: Anyone other than a DBA having access to Clear Global Cache. There is a page in Functional Administrator that allows a user to essentially bounce the forms server. Ask a DBA or the manager of the DBA group if those that have access to the Functional Administrator responsibility would be authorized to bounce the Apache server. If they say 'no' then you have your example…

Possible Finding language:

Following is potential language to document your finding:

Observation:

19 users have access to one more of these seeded responsibilities:

- Application Developer
- Functional Administrator

- Functional Developer
- System Administration
- System Administrator
- User Management
- SFM System Administrator

See detail in Appendix B for the full detail

Risk:

Excessive access to IT functions that related to user provisioning, system administration, profile options, security objects (such as Menus, Request Groups, and Responsibilities), development objects (Functions, Forms, Executables, Concurrent Programs), and other high risk IT functionality. This could lead to the following:

- Inappropriate or unapproved changes to data including security and development data as a result of lack of training or oversight
- Segregation of duties violations – for example: development objects are registered in Production by the same person doing the development – see IIA GTAG 2 which suggests that development objects should not be migrated to Prod via the development group. Implied is that these objects should be registered by someone other than the development group to maintain this SoD. Of greater risk is that developer access to Prod could change the definition of one or more development objects to change the functionality that could be achieved via that object.
- Currently none of the security or development objects are being audited via a trigger-based auditing solution so no quality assurance process is yet implemented. Therefore, unapproved changes could be happening in Prod with no process to detect them.
- Lack of peer review for development changes

Recommendation:

Security, development, support, IT compliance and DBA functions in the IT department need to be segregated. A risk assessment should be performed for all the major functions within these responsibilities and IT needs to determine who is authorized to make changes in Prod. While there could be overlap between these functions, risks exist if they do. Ultimately, only those authorized to make changes in

Prod should have access to the functions. Segregating the development of these changes from those that move the changes to a test environment and to Prod should also be a priority. In the role redesign process, we recommend each role in the organization have a Support role and a Configuration role. The Support role would include functions that are day to day and that don't go through the formal IT change management process. This does not mean there are no approvals, but that it doesn't have to go through the formal procedure of the change management process. One

Level of Effort:

Medium

Priority:

High

Chapter 23: OV-21 Instance strategy

Background:

Many organizations fail to understand risks in non-production environments or fail to properly address these risks. In this chapter, we seek to address management's understanding and implementation of addresses risks related to non-production environments.

Risk:

Failure to document and implement a proper instance strategy could lead to:

- Access to sensitive data in non-Prod environments
- Unsuccessful testing in non-Prod UAT environments because of inappropriate or unrecognized changes
- Users could decrypt passwords based on information accessed in non-Prod environments and use those passwords to log in as those users in Prod.

Control Description:

Organization has developed, documented, and implemented a security strategy for each instance. This includes the documentation of how security will be administered for each instance and how sensitive data will be protected.

Testing procedure:

Internal Controls Questionnaire

Comments related to testing:

Testing should be easy for this. Most organizations do not have a documented instance strategy. If they have addressed some of these risks, they should be documented.

Possible Finding language:

Following is potential language to document your finding:

Observation:

Organization has not documented (or implemented or fully implemented) an instance strategy that addresses (or fully addresses) risks related to:

- Decryption of passwords
- Protecting sensitive data
- Protecting the integrity of the system to allow for proper testing of changes

Risk:

Failure to document and implement a proper instance strategy could lead to:

- Access to sensitive data in non-Prod environments
- Unsuccessful testing in non-Prod UAT environments because of inappropriate or unrecognized changes
- Users could decrypt passwords based on information accessed in non-Prod environments and use those passwords to log in as those users in Prod.

Recommendation:

Organization should document a security by instance strategy that acknowledges the different uses of each instance, addresses the different risks, and defines the security policies for each instance.

An example would be the scrambling of sensitive data in non-prod instances in less secure instances like a development instance.

Organization should verify whether or not storage of passwords has been changed from encryption to hashing. See MOS Note: Note: 457166.1.

Level of Effort:

High

Priority:

High

Chapter 24: OV-22 Configuration Change Management policy

Background:

I alluded to this topic in the chapter above related to IT department role design. In that chapter, I addressed primarily the access to typical IT functions. In this chapter, I seek to address functional configurations. IT organizations often do a good job at designing policies and procedures related to 'development' changes – that is changes that need development or what I call object-oriented changes. Those changes follow an SDLC process. Development is first done in a development instance then migrated by a group independent of those doing the development to a test environment for user acceptance testing. The same group then migrates the development to production. Sometimes the objects are managed via a code management tool and migrated from Dev to Test to Prod via a code migration tool. However, organizations often fail to follow these same principles for 'development' that is not object-oriented.

What really is the intent of the change management process? Is it only to protect object-oriented development or should the same level of care be applied to changes that are made through forms or pages (i.e. configurations)?

I break the change management process into four buckets:

- Object-oriented development
- Patching cycles
- Security changes
- Configuration changes

Each of these types of changes have their own distinct characteristics. In this chapter, we are addressing the Configuration Change Management process.

What I first look for in a Configuration Change Management process is whether a risk assessment has been performed that identifies which configurations should be subject to the change management process. We will address more specific risks in the next chapter.

Risk:

Inappropriate or unauthorized changes to configurations that impact the way the system works or the controls designed.

Examples include:

- Payables Options
- Journal Sources
- Receivables Transaction Types
- OM Transaction Types
- Adjustment Approval Limits
- Accounting Rules
- Flexfield Values
- Security Rules
- Cross-Validation Rules
- Invoice Hold and Release Names

Control Description:

A risk assessment has been performed that identifies which configurations are subject to the change management process.

Testing procedure:

Internal Controls Questionnaire

Comments related to testing:

This should be fairly straight forward to test. Either they have a risk assessment that documents what they expect to go through the change management process or they don't. Having a risk assessment is essential for security design. As part of the security design, only those that are authorized to have access to these configurations should have access in Prod.

Possible Finding language:

Following is potential language to document your finding:

Observation:

There is no defined Configuration Change Management process for application configurations. Security related to these changes is inconsistently developed. Often end users have access to such forms when such forms should be isolated to IT personnel.

Risk:

Inappropriate or unauthorized changes to configurations that impact the way the system works or the controls designed.

Examples include:

- Payables Options (AP)
- Journal Sources (GL)
- Receivables Transaction Types (AR)
- Adjustment Approval Limits (AR)
- Accounting Rules (AR)
- System Options (AR)
- Document Types (PO)
- Line Types (PO)
- Flexfield Values (Common)
- Security Rules (Common)
- Cross-Validation Rules (Common)
- Invoice Hold and Release Names (AP)

Recommendation:

A risk assessment has been performed that identifies which configurations are subject to the change management process. As part of the risk assessment, the role(s) that is authorized to make the changes in Prod should be identified. Role-based security should be designed and implemented to grant access to such functions to only those that are authorized to make changes in Prod.

Level of Effort:

High

Priority:

High

Chapter 25: OV-23 Excessive access to configurations subject to the Change Management process

Background:

In the prior chapter, we sought to address whether or not the organization has performed a risk assessment to identify the configurations that should be subject to the risk assessment process. In this chapter, we seek to identify specific Functions where there is excessive access (i.e. people have access that are not authorized make changes in Prod).

Risk:

Users making changes to configurations in Production that should be subject to the change management process or that are not properly authorized.

Control Description:

Security has been designed to restrict access for these configurations to just those that are authorized to make the changes in Production.

Testing procedure:

Query 12: High Risk Single Functions

Comments related to testing:

The functions identified in the prior chapter have been included in Query 12. This will allow you to test, on a sample basis, functions that I'd expect to go through the change management process. I picked a cross section of functions that have likely have significant risk for your organization. Some of the functions (Flexfield Values, Security Rules, and Cross-Validation Rules) may not necessarily go through the change management process, but should have some type of control over changes. See comments in Chapter 17: OV-15 Chart of accounts maintenance which maintenance is done through the Flexfield Values function.

Possible Finding language:

Following is potential language to document your finding:

Observation:

Security related to Configurations that should be subject to the change management process has not been properly developed (or not developed consistently with the risk assessment associated with the Configuration Change Management policy). Therefore, there are users who have access to functions that should be subject to the change management process.

Risk:

Users making changes to configurations in Production that should be subject to the change management process or that are not properly authorized.

Recommendation:

All configurations that have the impact of changes the way the underlying code works should be subject to the change management process and be segregated in their own responsibility – one per module. For example:

- ABC AP Configuration
- ABC AR Configuration
- ABC GL Configuration

A detailed risk assessment should be documented that identifies each configuration that should be subject to the change management procedures, who can approve such changes, and what role is authorized to migrate such changes to production.

Access to the configuration roles should only be granted on a temporary basis when a change ticket is approved.

Level of Effort:

High

Priority:

High

Chapter 26: OV-24 Employees with more than one User

Background:

This chapter focuses on looking for an employee record that more than one User account. The system allows it and the existence of this scenario would be unusual. I developed this query looking for anomalies in the User data and have identified various reasons for this to exist. An employee record is associated with a User in the Person field as follows:

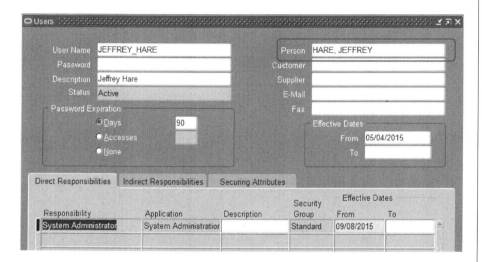

A second User referencing the same employee could look something like the following:

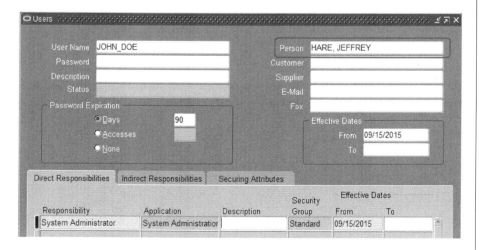

The existence of a second User account referring to the same employee could represent:

- A fictitious account setup to hide the identity of transactions (since the User Name is what shows up in the record history)
- A generic User account
- A 'delegate' ID where an admin or delegate is authorized to transact or approve on behalf of someone else (although this is done more elegantly through other means such as Worklist Access)

These are some example of purposes for second User accounts I have encountered.

Risk:

Maintenance of data through an account for which the employee is not accountable / use of generic accounts for maintenance.

Control Description:

Each employee, temporary workers, and contractor should only have one User account unless management approves the use of a generic account for a proper business purpose.

Testing procedure:

Query 9: Employees with more than one User

Comments related to testing:

When setting up a User, a Security Administrator typically associates an employee with the account. This links certain information in HR (Job, Position, Supervisor, Department and Email Address) to the User for functionality such as workflow notifications, approvals, and derivation of departments to which to charge expenses). The system allows more than one User to be associated with an employee.

Following is an example:

User 1:

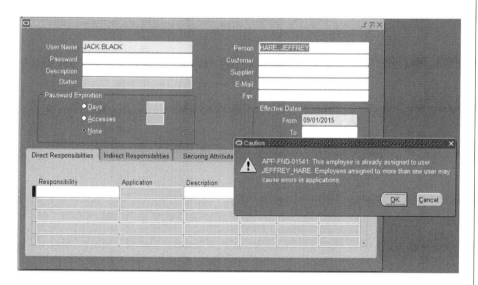

User 2:

Below is the message a Security Administrator receives when trying to associate the same employee to a second User:

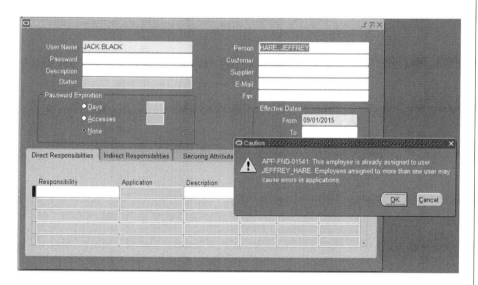

However, this is a 'soft warning.' It allows the second account to be created once you press "OK" to proceed. The second account looks 'normal', but probably would violate most organization's policies.

The one instance I have seen this used relates to the iExpense account where a designee is allowed to enter expenses on behalf of another person like where an Administrative Assistance enters an Expense Report for an executive. If that case, a primary login was used to enter their own expense report and a second login was used to enter the expense report on behalf of another user. However, my understanding is there is a more preferred way of delegating the ability to enter expenses reports to another person through the Expenses Preferences page.

So... I have yet to find a valid example where a second login is necessary.

If you find data in Query 9, inquire as to why and evaluate their response. If you have a scenario you want to run by me, email me at jhare@erpra.net.

Possible Finding language:

Following is potential language to document your finding:

Observation:

One or more employees have more than one User account associated with their employee record. This is unusual and could be an indication that a second account is set up for an employee to use.

It could also be an indication that one of the accounts is a generic user.

Risk:

Lack of accountability by a second User account associated with an employee. This could also be an indication of a generic user account which, again, could be used to obfuscate activity within the applications. This scenario could be a violation of the organization's policy.

Recommendation:

Organization should review the purpose of these and take action(s) necessary to bring them into compliance with their policy. It may also be necessary to set up monitoring related to one or more of these User accounts if it is a generic user.

Level of Effort:

Low

Priority:

Medium to High

Chapter 27: Internal Controls Questionnaire

Gaining an understanding of the Organization's E-Business Suite environment

Start with the following questions:

1. What is the version of the applications your organization is running?
2. What applications are your organization using within Oracle E-Business Suite?
3. When did your organization first implement the Suite and what was the original version you implemented?
4. If your organization isn't on the version you implemented, when was the latest upgrade performed to the version you are currently using?
5. Explain any third party relationships you have with the hosting or support of the applications.
6. What organization(s) was your original system integrator (i.e. helped implement the applications) or helped with your most recent upgrade if you have upgrade since your original implementation?

Evaluation of responses

1. What is the version of the applications your organization is running?

   Common answers: 11.5.10, 12.1.3, 12.2.3, 12.2.4. The major release most commonly used are 11.5.10 (also referred to as 11i). Release 12 is really two sub-releases. Oracle introduced the concept of on-line patching in release 12.2. Because of the significant technical difference between 12.1 and 12.2, Oracle has stated they will support the 12.1 and 12.2 as separate releases. I expect that a significant percentage or organizations will remain on 12.1 (which is current at 12.1.3), especially smaller organizations and organizations that don't run 24x7 operations.

2. What applications are your organization using within Oracle E-Business Suite?

Common answers: Varies depending on the nature of the organization. More commonly used modules include: General Ledger, Payables, Purchasing, Cash Management, Assets, Order Management, Inventory, Cost Management, Work in Process, Bill of Materials, Quality, Human Resources, Payroll, Advanced Benefits, and Advanced Collections. There are dozens more...

3. When did your organization first implement the Suite and what was the original version you implemented?

   Common answers: 10.7, 11, 11i, 12.1, 12.2 (or some point release within like 11.5.10 (11i) or 12.1.3).

4. If your organization isn't on the version you implemented, when was the latest upgrade performed to the version you are currently using?

   Common answers: We implemented on 11i and recently upgraded from 11i to 12.2.3 (or 12.1.3). Or... We implemented in 12.1.3 or 12.2.x (12.2.2, 12.2.4, etc.)

5. Explain any third party relationships you have with the hosting or support of the applications.

   Common answers: We are hosted by Oracle or x hosting company. We use x company to support our organization. We use x company to manage the applications (DBA support).

6. What organization(s) was your original system integrator (i.e. helped implement the applications) or helped with your most recent upgrade if you have upgrade since your original implementation?

These answers give you a feel for the environment.

Internal Controls Questionnaire (ICQ)

Following is an Internal Control Questionnaire with comments on what to expect and common answers.

Following are questions to pose to the client to support the SQL scripts run as part of an audit support engagement:

Overall IT General Controls

1. Have you read and complied with the recommendations in Oracle's Secure Configuration Guide (MOS Note 403537.1 for R12 / 189367.1 for 11i)? Are there any recommendations you chose not to implement? If so, why? Has anyone verified the steps taken to comply with the document? Are you familiar with the concept of Sensitive Administrative Pages that allow SQL injection and/or Operating System scripts to be executed from within them? How have you addressed these risks? Has management been presented and accepted the residual risks related to these forms and pages?

2. Have you read and complied with Oracle DMZ Configuration Guide (389490.1 for R12, 287176.1 for 11i)? Are there any recommendations you chose not to implement? If so, why? Has anyone verified the steps taken to comply with the document?

Application Security Design

3. Has security been developed based on the principle of least privilege – that is access for users has been designed and implemented to provide them with the minimum security to do their jobs?

4. Has a risk assessment been performed to determine which configurations should be subject to the change management process? Have those configurations been documented in a change management policy or have those configurations been isolated into their own role so that those that have access to such configurations know with certain which forms are subject to the change management process?

5. Related to Request Group design:

   a. Did you document which concurrent programs are high risk? Think about interface programs, conversion

programs, and reports with access to sensitive data (both custom and seeded)?
b. Was it clearly documented what constituted sensitive data and high risk concurrent programs from the beginning of the project? As custom programs were developed, was a list maintained as per the above example?
c. Were those that were responsible for approving custom request groups or use of seeded request groups in responsibilities aware of which reports contained sensitive data?
d. Were those responsible for approving changes to request groups aware of the high risk concurrent programs including those that contain sensitive data?

Password Parameters

6. Please provide the organization's policies related to the following password parameters:
   a. Minimum password length
   b. Complexity requirements – number, capitals, no repeating characters, no user name, symbols?
   c. Password Failure Limit (how many attempts before account is locked)
   d. No Reuse – how long or how many times before a password can be reused

Generic Users

7. Describe the circumstances that justify the use of a generic login (either seeded by the vendor or custom built by your organization).

8. Are 'owners' of generic users required to log the use of the generic user to justify its use?

9. Is there a system report that identifies when users log into the account that can be used to monitor the logins of generic users? Does someone monitor the report on a regular basis

and trace back the actual logins to the logs entered by the 'owner' of the generic login?

Change Management

10. Does the system log changes to data for changes that are subject to the Change Management process? Does this include object changes? Does this include security change? Does this include configuration changes?

11. Does someone independent of the change management process trace a list of actual changes taken from a system-based audit trail and trace such changes back to the approved changes to test for unapproved changes? If not, is there a way your organization tests for completeness of changes?

12. Are all changes to Profile Options subject to your change management process? If certain ones do not need approval in order to be change, are they documented? Are there certain profile options that should not be set in a Production environment? When a change to a profile option is requested, is it documented who or which group needs to approve such changes? Does the system build an audit history for changes to profile options?

13. Are users allowed to override profile options by setting them in the User Profile Values form (aka Personal Profile Values form or the Profile User Values function)? If yes, can they override any of them or just certain ones?

14. Please provide a list of IT users and identify their role in the organization.

Evaluation of responses

1. Have you read and complied with the recommendations in Oracle's Secure Configuration Guide (MOS Note 403537.1

for R12 / 189367.1 for 11i)? Are there any recommendations you chose not to implement? If so, why? Has anyone verified the steps taken to comply with the document? Are you familiar with the concept of Sensitive Administrative Pages that allow SQL injection and/or Operating System scripts to be executed from within them? How have you addressed these risks? Has management been presented and accepted the residual risks related to these forms and pages?

Audit procedure: If they say yes, ask them to provide evidence of the compliance. If they can't produce evidence, evaluate the results of Query 4 – related to Generic users. More than likely one or more generic users that Oracle says can be disabled are still active. Review the Responsibilities assigned to the user in Query 2 – Active Users and Assigned Responsibilities to identify which Responsibilities are assigned to the generic Users.

Audit procedure: Related to sensitive administration pages, most organizations have not addressed the risks by 1. Restricting access 2. Monitoring the activity in these forms through a trigger-based or log-based technology. There are always users who have access to these forms in Prod. The easiest way to test for access is to review Query 2 – Active Users and Assigned Responsibilities to identify if anyone has access to the Alert Manager responsibility. There is always at least one person. Typical findings would be that they haven't evaluated the risk and that they haven't address the recommendations in the Oracle MOS Note or documented acceptance of the residual risk by management.

2. Have you read and complied with Oracle DMZ Configuration Guide (389490.1 for R12, 287176.1 for 11i)? Are there any recommendations you chose not to implement? If so, why? Has anyone verified the steps taken to comply with the document?

Audit procedure: Evaluate their response. They may not be aware of the document or they may be aware and have taken some steps. If they have no internet facing applications this document will be not applicable. Typical internet facing applications would include iExpense, iSupplier, iStore, iProcurement, and iRecrutiment, or Employee Self Service.

Application Security Design

3. Has security been developed based on the principle of least privilege – that is access for users has been designed and implemented to provide them with the minimum security to do their jobs?

    Audit Procedure: Evaluate their response. Review role design via Query 1 – Responsibility Definitions.

    Following are examples of observations that could be used make the case that the principle of least privilege isn't being followed:

    - If you identify a user that have more than one Responsibility within a module (that aren't just Inquiry) – this is evidence because role based access control design would be to build a Responsibility that is specific to their role. Sometimes a Responsibility is built with access to several modules and sometimes a Responsibility is sub-Role (i.e. is built for appropriate access for the module).
    - Responsibilities are built using seeded Menus
    - Responsibility are built using seeded Request Groups
    - Responsibilities aren't built with a role name in it (such as Manager, Supervisor or Clerk)
    - One or more Responsibilities still have access to AZN menus – see Query 3 (note the risk of false positives)

    See more on AZN menus at this YouTube video:

    ERP Risk Advisors: AZN Menus Risks and Recommendations

https://www.youtube.com/watch?v=vdClsxHj9do which can be access at: www.YouTube.com/ERPRiskAdvisors.

I will admit this is perhaps the most difficult response to evaluate especially if you aren't familiar with role design concepts and aren't familiar with what are seeded Menus or seeded Request Groups

4. Has a risk assessment been performed to determine which configurations should be subject to the change management process? Have those configurations been documented in a change management policy or have those configurations been isolated into their own role so that those that have access to such configurations know with certain which forms are subject to the change management process?

   Audit Procedure: Evaluate response. Have the performed a risk assessment to determine which configurations are subject to the change management process and which ones haven't. They may say that everything goes through change control, but rarely is that the case. Evaluate role design in Query 1... MORE>>>

5. Related to Request Group design:

   a. Did you document which concurrent programs are high risk? Think about interface programs, conversion programs, and reports with access to sensitive data (both custom and seeded)?
   b. Was it clearly documented what constituted sensitive data and high risk concurrent programs from the beginning of the project? As custom programs were developed, was a list maintained as per the above example?
   c. Were those that were responsible for approving custom request groups or use of seeded request groups in responsibilities aware of which reports contained sensitive data?
   d. Were those responsible for approving changes to request groups aware of the high risk concurrent programs including those that contain sensitive data?

Password Parameters

6. Please provide the organization's policies related to the following password parameters:
   a. Minimum password length
   b. Complexity requirements – number, capitals, no repeating characters, no user name, symbols?
   c. Password Failure Limit (how many attempts before account is locked)
   d. No Reuse – how long or how many times before a password can be reused
   e. Number of days until password has to be changed?

   Audit Procedure: Compare the response to the above to the following profile option in Query 5 – Profile Options:
   • SignOn Password Failure Limit – default 0, recommend 3 - locks user account after failed logins
   • SignOn Password Hard to Guess – default no , recommend yes - 1 letter, 1 number, not repeating char, d/n include username
   • SignOn Password Length – default none, recommend 7
   • SignOn Password No Reuse – default 0, recommend 180 or more- # of days before password can be reused
   • SignOn Audit Level – default none, recommend Form
   • Password Case Option - recommend Sensitive – determines if password is case sensitive

   Note: None of these should be set at the User level. You should only find it set at the Site level. Sometimes you will find where it has been overridden at the User level

   Audit Procedure: Evaluate the 'Password expiration days' by reviewing the results of Query 11 -Users outside of Password Expiration Policy. If there are issues, recommend automating the default of this value by the following Personalization to the Users form.

Generic Users

7. Describe the circumstances that justify the use of a generic login (either seeded by the vendor or custom built by your organization).

   Audit Procedure: Evaluate response. Most organizations have policies against the use of a generic user for application maintenance. You will see the SYSADMIN user (seeded) used sometimes because they will say Oracle requires it. However, most of the time the same maintenance can be done using a named login through the System Administrator responsibility. Suggest that each time the generic user is used it needs to be logged and justified – and that all maintenance should first be attempted via their named login.

8. Are 'owners' of generic users required to log the use of the generic user to justify its use?

   Audit procedure: Evaluate their response. Make the recommendation that usage should be limited to just when required by the vendor and when the maintenance cannot be done through a named login.

9. Is there a system report that identifies when users log into the account that can be used to monitor the logins of generic users? Does someone monitor the report on a regular basis and trace back the actual logins to the logs entered by the 'owner' of the generic login?

   Audit procedure: Signon Audit reports (there are several, but the Signon Audit Users shows logins) can be used to pull a list of all logins related to any users. The report can be run for a specific user. Often the data gets purged, sometimes every 30 days so you may not be able to pull a large population. You could have them run the report for all users or just give them a list of generic users for which to run the report. The most commonly used seeded User is SYSADMIN. Identify the seeded generic users via Query 4 – Generic users and Query 6 – Possible Generic Users

Change Management

10. Does the system log changes to data for changes that are subject to the Change Management process? Does this include object changes? Does this include security change? Does this include configuration changes?

Audit Procedure: Evaluate the response. Most organizations do not have a GRC tool that builds the detailed audit history for such changes. Two common providers of such software are Oracle GRC (CCG module) and CaoSys CS*Audit – both solutions use triggers that need to be deployed table by table based on a risk assessment performed to identify what tables are being used and the risk associated with changes to the data. This is very different from SAP which has a transport process to move changes and logs the changes. Oracle has nothing similar to this and, therefore, there is no audit history available.

If they have one of these tools available, ask them for a report of what tables the tool is monitoring and how they identified the tables that needed to be monitored. It should include all tables related to development activities, security changes, configuration changes throughout the various modules these use, and all tables underlying forms that are identified in MOS 403537.1 (see first question above - and the related document 1334930.1 which provides a list of sensitive administration pages). If you are interested in some help here, send me the list of the tables they audit and I'll do a quick evaluation of how comprehensive is their auditing. (Email jhare@erpra.net). PCAOB is starting to become more aggressive at requiring a system based audit trail to test for completeness of the change management process (i.e. tracing actual changes pulled from system based audit trails back to the change management ticketing system to test for unauthorized changes).

11. Does someone independent of the change management process trace a list of actual changes taken from a system-based audit trail and trace such changes back to the approved changes to test for unapproved changes? If not, is there a way your organization tests for completeness of changes?

Audit procedure: Consider their response. If they say yes, ask for a system-based log. Evaluate the completeness of the changes. Ask what technology was used to build the logs. If it wasn't triggers described above, it could be database or network logs which have the pros / cons. Email me at jhare@erpra.net if you have questions about how to evaluate their response.

12. Are all changes to Profile Options subject to your change management process? If certain ones do not need approval in order to be change, are they documented? Are there certain profile options that should not be set in a Production environment? When a change to a profile option is requested, is it documented who or which group needs to approve such changes? Does the system build an audit history for changes to profile options?

Audit procedure: Evaluate their response. Ask for a document where a risk assessment has been documented. An example of a risk assessment related to Profile Options can be found on the Book Resources page at www.erpra.net.

The most important question is who should approve the changes – this should vary from profile option to profile option. For example, password related profile options (Signon Password Case) should be approved by the Chief Security Officer. A profile option that impact the Journal Approval process in the GL (GL: Journal Review Required) should be approved by the Controller. There are over 8000 profile options available to be set at the Site, Application, Responsibility, or User level.

Giving you the definitive list of all 'high risk' profile options is impossible. I have provided you a list in the Book Resources page on our website. However, this list should not be considered to be comprehensive. I recommend you develop your own list based on the profile options currently assigned in Prod. I will update the template as I identify those that should be considered high risk. I would also appreciate you sending me any that you believe should be added to the list so I can update the list. Let's collaborate to continue developing this list.

13. Are users allowed to override profile options by setting them in the User Profile Values form (aka Personal Profile Values form or the Profile User Values function)? If yes, can they override any of them or just certain ones?

Audit Procedure: Evaluate their response. Generally I don't recommend allowing any users to have access this form in Production. Find out more on this topic at:

ERP Risk Advisors: Profile Options - What are they and Why Auditors Should Care

https://www.youtube.com/watch?v=NGa_rGAetLc which can be access at: www.YouTube.com/ERPRiskAdvisors.

Chapter 28: Query 1: Active Responsibility Definitions

Purpose of the Query

Query 1 essentially provides you with the definitions of a Responsibility for those that are active (i.e. not end-dated). This query supports audit tests OV-3 and OV-9.

It provides a view into the most important aspects of how a Responsibility is defined – the Menu, Request Group, and Exclusions (Function and Menu)

Following is the form from which the data is accessed:

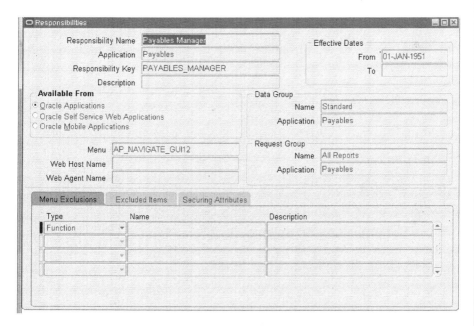

This query provides all the information you'd find in the 'Responsibilities' form – the definitions of all Responsibilities including the menu, request group, data group, and function / menu exclusions.

Evaluation of results
Sample data from Query 1: Responsibility Definitions

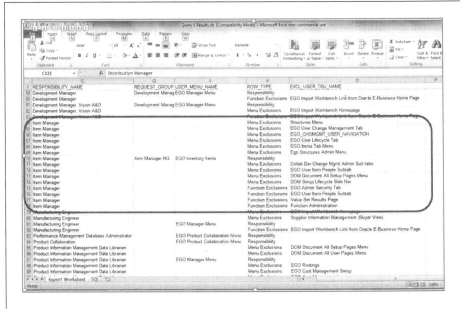

There is a lot of data provided in this query. I typically start by hiding all the columns other than what is visible above.

Next, I add three columns – one to identify whether the Responsibility is custom built (I use the header Custom?), one to identify if the custom Responsibilities use a standard menu (I use the header Std Menu?), and one to identify if the custom Responsibilities use a standard request group (I used the header Std RG?). To understand whether the naming conventions your organization uses. If you organization is "ABC Company" it may be that ABC is used at the beginning or end of a Responsibility name in order to identify it as custom. Usually from looking at the data, I can identify what the naming convention appears to be. Following is a list seeded responsibilities for the most commonly used modules:

Module	Seeded Responsibility Name
Advanced Supply Chain Planning	@Advanced Supply Chain Planner
Bills of Material	Bills of Material
CRM Foundation	CRM Administrator, Vision University
Cost Management	Cost Management
Engineering	Engineering
Human Resources	Global HRMS Manager
Inventory	Inventory
Advanced Product Catalog	Item Manager

Module	Seeded Responsibility Name
Manufacturing Scheduling	Manufacturing Scheduler
Master Scheduling/MRP	Material Planner
Inventory	Materials & Mfg
Marketing	Oracle Marketing Super User
Advanced Pricing	Oracle Pricing Manager, Global
Web Applications Desktop Integrator	Oracle Web ADI
Order Capture	Order Capture - Sales Manager
Order Management	Order Management Super User
Quality	Quality
Shipping Execution	Shipping
TeleSales	TeleSales
Work in Process	Work in Process
e-Commerce Gateway	e-Commerce Gateway
Payables	Payables Manager
Receivables	Receivables Manager
Cash Management	Cash Management
Assets	Asset Manager
Purchasing	Purchasing Super User
General Ledger	General Ledger Super User
Trade Management	Trade Management
Human Resources	US HR Manager US HRMS Manager US Payroll Manager
Trading Community Manager	Trading Community Manager

Additionally, following is a list of seeded Responsibilities that are core the application (i.e. not specific to a module):

System Administrator	Application Developer
System Administration	Functional Developer
Functional Administrator	Alert Manager
Workflow Administrator	User Management (derived from assignment of "Security Administrator" Role)
Workflow Administrator Event Manager	Workflow Administrator Web (New)
Workflow Administrator Web Applications	
Workflow User	Workflow User Web Applications

The list above is not meant to be exhaustive. If you are wondering if a Responsibility is seeded or custom email me at jhare@erpra.net and I'll do my best to help you.

Referring back to results for Query 1 (above) for the Responsibility "Item Manager" we can observe the following:

- The Request Group name is "Item Manager RG" – i.e. the use of seeded Request Groups
- The User Menu Name is EGO Inventory Items – i.e. the use of seeded Menus
- Lack of Function Exclusion for "Profile User Values"

Use of seeded Request Groups

We could draw a couple of conclusions and recommendations from this information. First, 'Item Manager RG' is likely a seeded request group (provided by Oracle) by noting the absence of 'ABC' at the beginning (or end) of this Request Group name is an indication that the request group is seeded.

The following is how you could document this…

Observation: It appears that Responsibility "Item Manager" is using a standard Request Group.

Risk: Use of standard (seeded) Request Groups usually indicate that access to concurrent programs and reports haven't been designed specific to the design of the Role. This likely results in the access by the Users who have this Responsibility having excessive access to high risk concurrent programs (i.e. Concurrent Programs that can process or change data) and/or excessive access to sensitive data).

Recommendation: We recommend that each Responsibility be designed with a custom Request Group that is built specific for the requirements by the Users to which the Responsibility is or will be assigned.

You may also want to find some examples to point out. For example, the "All Reports" Request Group for the Purchasing module has access to the following high risk concurrent programs:

- Catalog Data Purge
- Purge Catalog interMedia Index
- Purge Purchasing Open Interface Processed Data
- Purge System Saved Requisition

Tip: query for concurrent programs like 'Purge' 'Interface' 'Update' 'Decrypt' 'Program' 'Conversion' and 'Process'. Inevitably you will find some of these programs that update data in an Inquiry Responsibility or a Purge process that is widely available. Use these to illustrate the risks.

A working list of sample high risk concurrent programs to use in your report is published at the Book Resources section at www.erpra.net.

Use of Seeded Menus

Similar to the use of seeded Request Groups, we could draw the same conclusion related to use seeded Menus. In reviewing the Menu name, which is "EGO Inventory Items", we could recognize it isn't a custom Menu because it doesn't have 'ABC' in the name (or something that would indicate it is custom Menu.

The following is how you could document this...

Observation: We have identified one or more custom Responsibilities that use a seeded Menu in its development.

Risks: The use of seeded Menus leaves your organization subject to upgrade risk. Please see findings related Query 3: AZN menus as an example of why you should not use a seeded Menu in the development of a custom Responsibility.

Recommendation: We recommend that each custom Responsibility is built which a custom Menu that reflects the needs of the Role for which the Responsibility is built. Each Responsibility should be built on the principle of least privilege which means that only it only includes the Privileges, Functions, and Concurrent Programs that are necessary to perform the processes for each of the Users to which it is assigned.

Lack of Function Exclusion for the high risk Function "Profile User Values"

Finally, from looking at the Function Exclusions, we observe that the Function 'Profile User Values' is not excluded. This Function is contained in nearly every standard Menu so we could make a recommendation that it be excluded from the responsibility ASAP and that it not be included in any custom Menu or custom Responsibility in the future.

See more on the risks related to the 'Profile User Values' functions on our You Tube channel you can access at www.erpra.net.

I will address more on the subject of high risk Functions is Query 12.

There are additional high risk Functions that we will address in that chapter.

Query 1 SQL Statement: Active Responsibility Definitions

```
SELECT  application_name,
    application_short_name,
    responsibility_name,
    resp_desc,
    responsibility_id,
    request_group_id,
    request_group_name,
    menu_name,
    user_menu_name,
    menu_id,
    row_type,
    row_type_idx,
    excl_obj_id,
    excl_obj_name,
    excl_user_obj_name

FROM

    (SELECT 'Responsibility' row_type,
        1 row_type_idx        ,
        a.application_short_name  ,
        a.application_name        ,
        rv.responsibility_name    ,
        rv.description resp_desc  ,
        r.responsibility_id       ,
        r.request_group_id        ,
        rg.request_group_name     ,
        m1.menu_name              ,
        mv1.user_menu_name        ,
        m1.menu_id                ,
        TO_NUMBER (NULL) excl_obj_id,
        '' excl_obj_name          ,
        '' excl_user_obj_name

FROM    apps.fnd_responsibility r    ,
        apps.fnd_responsibility_tl rv,
        apps.fnd_menus m1            ,
        apps.fnd_menus_vl mv1        ,
        apps.fnd_application_vl a    ,
        apps.fnd_request_groups rg


WHERE   rv.responsibility_id = r.responsibility_id
        AND r.end_date IS NULL
        AND m1.menu_id          = r.menu_id
        AND mv1.menu_id         = m1.menu_id
        AND a.application_id    = r.application_id
        AND rg.application_id(+)  = r.application_id
        AND rg.request_group_id(+) = r.request_group_id

UNION ALL

SELECT 'Function Exclusions' row_type,
```

```
                 2 row_type_idx               ,
                 a.application_short_name      ,
                 a.application_name            ,
                 rv.responsibility_name        ,
                 rv.description resp_desc       ,
                 r.responsibility_id           ,
                 TO_NUMBER(NULL) request_group_id,
                 '' request_group_name          ,
                 '' menu_name                   ,
                 '' user_menu_name              ,
                 TO_NUMBER(NULL) menu_id        ,
                 f.function_id excl_obj_id       ,
                 f.function_name excl_obj_name  ,
                 fv.user_function_name excl_user_obj_name

FROM    apps.fnd_resp_functions rf   ,
          apps.fnd_responsibility r    ,
          apps.fnd_responsibility_vl rv,
          apps.fnd_form_functions f    ,
          apps.fnd_form_functions_vl fv,
          apps.fnd_application_vl a

WHERE  rf.rule_type       = 'F'
       AND f.function_id      = rf.action_id
       AND fv.function_id     = f.function_id
       AND r.responsibility_id = rf.responsibility_id
       AND r.end_date IS NULL
       AND rv.responsibility_id = r.responsibility_id
       AND a.application_id     = r.application_id

UNION ALL

SELECT 'Menu Exclusions' row_type      ,
          1 row_type_idx                ,
          a.application_short_name       ,
          a.application_name            ,
          rv.responsibility_name         ,
          rv.description resp_desc        ,
          r.responsibility_id            ,
          TO_NUMBER(NULL) request_group_id,
          '' request_group_name          ,
          '' menu_name                   ,
          '' user_menu_name              ,
          TO_NUMBER(NULL) menu_id        ,
          m.menu_id excl_obj_id          ,
          m.menu_name excl_obj_name      ,
          mv.user_menu_name excl_menu_obj_name

FROM    apps.fnd_resp_functions rf   ,
          apps.fnd_responsibility r    ,
          apps.fnd_responsibility_vl rv,
          apps.fnd_menus m             ,
          apps.fnd_menus_vl mv         ,
```

```
                apps.fnd_application_vl a

        WHERE  rf.rule_type      = 'M'
          AND m.menu_id          = rf.action_id
          AND mv.menu_id         = m.menu_id
          AND r.responsibility_id = rf.responsibility_id
          AND r.end_date IS NULL
          AND rv.responsibility_id = r.responsibility_id
          AND a.application_id    = r.application_id      )
ORDER BY 1,3,12
```

Chapter 29: Query 2: Active Users and their Assigned Responsibilities

Purpose of the Query

Query 2 gives active Users and their currently assigned Responsibilities. It does not report Users who have been end-dated or Responsibilities that have been end-dated for Users that are still active. This query supports audit tests OV-3, OV-5, OV-9, OV-19, and OV-20.

The purpose of this query is to give insight into what Users are active and what Responsibilities are assigned to these active Users. This query provides you visibility to all active Users and their currently assigned Responsibilities. There are lots of observations and conclusions we could draw from this information.

One thing we are looking for is the number of users that have access to high risk seeded responsibilities such as System Administrator, Application Developer, and Alert Manager. Since all of these seeded responsibilities contain access to security and development objects that are subject to approval and the change management process, we typically like to see this limited to just a couple of employees or better yet custom responsibilities designed based on RBAC principles.

Following is the form from which the data is accessed:

The above shows you the data in the Users form. This is the main form where administration of Users and Responsibility assignments are made. Users can also be set up and administered through the User Management module. To the extent that a Responsibility is assigned via a Role through the user of the User Management module this query picks up the 'Indirect Responsibilities' assigned as shown below.

Users						

User Name SYSADMIN   **Person**
Password   **Customer**
Description System Administrator   **Supplier**
Status Active   **E-Mail**

Password Expiration   **Fax**

○ Days 90
● Accesses   Effective Dates
● None   From 01/01/1951
                          To

		Security	Effective Dates	
Responsibility	Application	Group	From	To
Application Diagnostics	Application Object Library	Standard	01/01/1951	
Application Diagnostics	Application Object Library	Standard	05/01/2015	07/17/2015
Integrated SOA Gateway	Application Object Library	Standard	10/14/2005	
Integrated SOA Gateway	Application Object Library	Standard	10/07/2005	
Integration Repository	Application Object Library	Standard	10/14/2005	05/13/2014

Record: 9/13   <OSC>

Note: in this version of the book, we do not have procedures or queries related to the User Management module where Roles are assigned to a user. In subsequent versions, we may add more procedures to address such risks. However, in most organizations 95% or more (and in some cases 100%) of the access assignments are done directly through assigning Responsibilities rather than using User Management to assign Roes.

Develop custom responsibilities to split apart System Administrator, Application Developer, Functional Administrator, Functional Developer, Alert Manager, and System Administration. For all the responsibilities, have management identify the employees that are specifically authorized to make the changes. In most organizations, we typically we find a primary and a backup employee, resulting in no more than two employees who have access to these functions.

Alert Manager is a responsibility that contains the Alerts form. The Alerts form is a form that allows ad hoc SQL statements and OS scripts to be executed from within it. As such we highly recommend a trigger-based auditing tool be implemented that both audits the data in it and notifies appropriate personnel when the form is used.

Evaluation of results
Sample data from Query 2: Active Users and Their Responsibilities

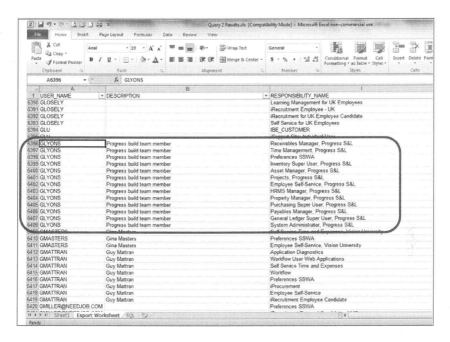

There are several things we look at in this query:

- Users with access to one or more seeded powerful
  responsibilities. In the example above GLYONS has access to
  Receivables Manager, Inventory Super User, Asset Manager,
  HRMS Manager, Purchasing Super User, Payables Manager,
  General Ledger Super User, and System Administrator – all of
  which essentially have full access to all functionality in these
  modules. This is an indication of serious risks and
  Segregation of Duties issues.

Another way to look at this data is through the use of pivot tables:

The above shows a Pivot Table with the Responsibilities and the number of assigned Users.

	A	B
1	Drop Report Filter Fields Here	
2		
3	Count of RESPONSIBILITY_NAME	
4	USER_NAME	Total
5	DATAMERGE	182
6	OPERATIONS	136
7	MFG	131
8	EBUSINESS	123
9	JPALMER	107
10	RETAIL	100
11	PROCESS_OPS	100
12	PSTOCKMAN	89
13	WTUCKER	88
14	SSCNEWALL	83
15	GERMANY	77
16	PROJMFG	73
17	NETHERLANDS	73
18	SERVICES	71
19	PROCESS	70
20	UK	67
21	GUEST	65
22	SWEDEN	63
23	FRANCE	63
24	BELGIUM	61
25	PJM	60
26	JKBOWERS	60
27	CMOORE	59
28	FRODRIGUES	58
29	ITALY	57
30	AMRBUILDTEAM	56

REsps | **Users** | Detail | SQL

The above shows a Pivot Table summarizing Users and the number of Responsibilities assigned to each User, descending by the number of assigned Responsibilities (showing the User with the largest number of assigned Responsibilities).

In this case, I developed a Pivot Table that counts the number of users that have access to each responsibility.

I look for access to responsibilities that should be tightly controlled because they are security related, should be subject to change management process, or have access to forms that allow SQL statements. In the case above, we can note that there are 83 assignments of the Alert Manager responsibility. We'd expect to see this responsibility only assigned to two or three people.

Another thing we look at in the context of this pivot table is access to seeded responsibilities. There are only a few cases where we'd recommend assigning seeded responsibilities. A couple of examples where this is acceptable would be: Employee Self Service, Manager Self Service, iProcurement, and iExpense where the functionality of the responsibilities is very limited and the risk of assigning the standard responsibility is negligible. The rest of the responsibilities that are assigned to users should all be custom and, therefore, in our example start with ABC. To the extent that seeded responsibilities are assigned to users, you should have a discussion with management as to why – and why they haven't developed custom responsibilities that are Role–based.

Having an org chart of the IT organization would be helpful to analyze the results. Another way to gather this information is to use an Internal Controls Questionnaire.

Following are some of the more common Observations, Risks, and Recommendations that come from this query:

Observation:

There are 14 people that have access to Alert Manager.

Risk:

Alert Manager is a Responsibility that allows for the execution of ad hoc SQL statements and Operating System scripts. A user with access to this in Prod can execute any SQL statement that a DBA would using the 'APPS' login including both DML and DDL commands. Inherently, Oracle does not provide any tracking of changes made through this form. This means a User with access to this form could embed and execute a SQL statement or Operating System script then delete the record – effectively covering their tracks.

Recommendation:

Because of the extreme risks of this form, access should be limited to no more than two people who are authorized to make changes in Production. All changes made through this form should be subject to the change management process including through a peer review process. A trigger or log-based solution should be deployed to build a complete audit history of all DML activity within this form (Inserts, Updates, and Deletes). Such audit trail should be protected from being tampered with by the Users who have access to make such changes in Production. Additionally, the trigger- or log-based solution should have a process that immediately notifies an IT change management auditor when such a change in made in Production. Finally, a quality assurance process should be in place that traces actual changes from the secure repository of changes back to the approved changes (change management ticketing system). The quality assurance process should test for unapproved changes as well as for the accuracy of the changes (i.e. the change that was tested and peer-reviewed was the change made and the only change made).

Ok… so we've addressed one of the over 50 forms that allow SQL injection or an Operating System script to be executed from within it. We'll have more on this topic later in Query 12.

Next topic… change management within the IT organization

Another analysis I like to do based on this query is to review how many Users have access to the following Responsibilities:

- System Administrator
- System Administrator
- Application Developer
- Functional Administrator
- Functional Developer
- User Management (derived from assignment of Security Administrator role in the User Management module)

What I typically do is isolate the assignments and identify how many users have access to these Responsibilities. Combined, these make up the access that you'd expect to be granted to the following roles:

- DBAs
- Security Administrators
- Developers (or whomever is authorized to move development work to Production)

After getting a complete list of employees, I ask if all the employees have access to all the Functions assigned to them are authorized to make changes through the forms in Production. Inevitably, the client will relent and admit that there are many Users that have access to one or more of the forms in those Responsibilities for which they are not authorized to make changes in Prod. The root cause of this is a lack of proper role design within the IT organization.

Following are a few thoughts on this topic:

1. Ask IT management if developers are authorized to make changes in Production. Aren't developers supposed to be kept from making changes in Production? Why would you enforce that through the object-oriented development and not through changes such as registering Executables and Concurrent Programs, developing Alerts and Personalizations, or Workflow development?
2. Ask a DBA if those that have access to System Administrator are authorized to Concurrent Managers which are a part of that Responsibility.
3. Ask a Security Administrator if a DBA is authorized to make changes to Menus, Request Groups, and Responsibilities which are found in the Security Administrator responsibility.
4. Ask a DBA if those that have access to Functional Administrator (typically developers) are authorizing to clear the java cache (similar to bouncing the application server).

This leads to the following:

Observation

There are Users who have access to one or more Forms and pages in the following responsibilities of which they are not authorized to make changes in Production:

- System Administrator
- System Administrator
- Application Developer
- Functional Administrator
- Functional Developer
- User Management

Risk

Unauthorized changes to data through one or more of the forms or pages in Production.

Recommendation

IT management needs perform a risk assessment through which they identify the group that is authorized to make changes through each of the forms that are accessible through those Responsibilities named above. Those that make changes in Production should be separate from those that do the development. Someone independent of those that make the changes in Production should perform a quality assurance role related to the changes.

IT management needs to re-design Responsibilities based on the above risk. Each role should be built on the principle of least privilege – that is should only have access to the forms and pages through which they are authorized to change the data in Production.

Next topic… role design

This is probably the most difficult topic to write about in this whole book because it is the most complicated topic. I'll start with the Observation, Risk, and Recommendation in summary and my best to explain how to present a credible Finding related to this topic.

Observation

Application security wasn't built based on Role-based Access Control (RBAC) principles.

Risk

Excessive access to high risk single Functions, Excessive access to sensitive data, and Segregation of Duties violations.

Recommendations

Roles need to be re-designed based on RBAC principles and the principle of least privilege.

In subsequent versions of this book I will write more about findings related to Role Design. As I wrote in Chapter 5: OV-3 Role design, the best approach to testing role design is to run a SaaS service like CS*Proviso from CaoSys or using installed software like CS*Comply from CaoSys – both solutions use content I have been developing for over 10 years.

Query 2 SQL Statement: Active Users and their Assigned Responsibilities

```
SELECT  u.user_name
,       u.description
,       u.start_date              user_start_date
,       u.end_date                user_end_date
,       u. employee_id            user_employee_id
,       u. password_lifespan_days           user_password_expiration_days
,       a.application_name
,       a.application_short_name
,       r.responsibility_name
,       r.responsibility_key
,       r.responsibility_id
,       r.start_date              resp_start_date
,       r.end_date                resp_end_date
,       rg.start_date            assignment_start_date
,       rg.expiration_date       assignment_end_date
FROM  (
    SELECT  wur.user_name
    ,       wur.role_orig_system_id
    ,       (   SELECT application_id
                FROM apps.fnd_application
                WHERE application_short_name =
                    REPLACE(SUBSTR( wur.role_name
                    ,       INSTR(wur.role_name, '|', 1, 1)+1
                    ,       (INSTR(wur.role_name, '|', 1, 2)-INSTR(wur.role_name,
'|', 1, 1)-1))
                    ,       '%col', ':')) resp_appl_id
    ,       wur.start_date
    ,       wur.expiration_date
    FROM  apps.wf_local_user_roles    wur
    WHERE   wur.role_orig_system = 'FND_RESP'
    AND     NOT wur.role_name LIKE 'FND_RESP|%|ANY'
    AND     wur.partition_id = 2
    AND     (((wur.start_date is NULL) OR (TRUNC(SYSDATE) >=
TRUNC(wur.start_date)))
    AND     ((wur.expiration_date IS NULL) OR (TRUNC(SYSDATE) <
trunc(wur.expiration_date)))
    AND     ((wur.user_start_date IS NULL) OR (TRUNC(SYSDATE) >=
trunc(wur.user_start_date)))
    AND     ((wur.user_end_date IS NULL) OR (TRUNC(SYSDATE) <
trunc(wur.user_end_date)))
    AND     ((wur.role_start_date IS NULL) OR (TRUNC(SYSDATE) >=
TRUNC(wur.role_start_date)))
    AND     ((wur.role_end_date IS NULL) OR (TRUNC(SYSDATE) <
trunc(wur.role_end_date))))) rg
    ,       apps.fnd_user u
    ,       apps.fnd_responsibility_vl r
    ,       apps.fnd_application_vl a
WHERE   u.user_name = rg.user_name
AND     r.responsibility_id = rg.role_orig_system_id
AND     r.application_id = rg.resp_appl_id
AND     a.application_id = r.application_id
```

Chapter 30: Query 3: Users with AZN Menus

Purpose of the Query

Returns users with AZN menus still assigned, but only at top level of menu. This query supports audit test OV-8.

Following is an example of a menu containing an AZN menu:

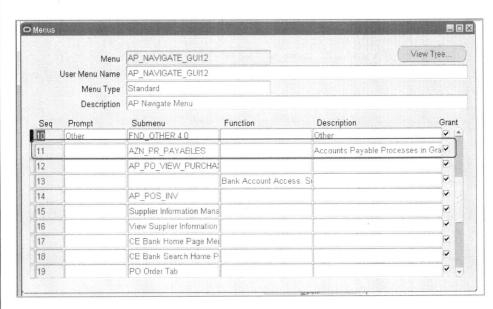

Following is an example of an AZN menu:

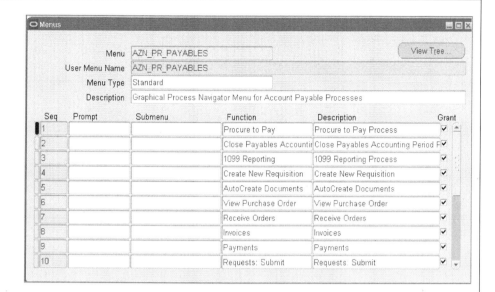

Following shows all the Functions contained in the AZN_PR_PAYABLES menu:

Seq	Prompt	Submenu	Function	Description
1			Procure to Pay	Procure to Pay Process
2			Close Payables Accounting Period	Close Payables Accounting Period Process
3			1099 Reporting	1099 Reporting Process
4			Create New Requisition	Create New Requisition
5			AutoCreate Documents	AutoCreate Documents
6			View Purchase Order	View Purchase Order
7			Receive Orders	Receive Orders
8			Invoices	Invoices
9			Payments	Payments
10			Requests: Submit	Requests: Submit
11			Payment Batches	Payment Batches
12			AP Accounting Periods	AP Accounting Periods
13			Suppliers	Suppliers
14		AP_APXINWKB_MENU		
15		Supplier Information Management (Buyer View)		

Evaluation of results
Sample data from Query 3: AZN Menus

	USER_NAME	RESPONSIBILITY_NAME	USER_MENU_NAME	AZN_MENU_NAME
1	USER_NAME	RESPONSIBILITY_NAME	USER_MENU_NAME	AZN_MENU_NAME
2	AAMBROS	Receivable Role UK	AR_NAVIGATE_GUI_NO_IEX	AZN_PR_RECEIVABLES
3	ABOASE	General Ledger, UK Health Services	GL_SUPERUSER	AZN_PR_GL
4	ABOASE	General Ledger, UK Health Services - Divisional Directors A	GL_SUPERUSER	AZN_PR_GL
5	ABOASE	Inventory Progress UK Super User	INV_NAVIGATE	AZN_PR_ATO
6	ABOASE	Inventory Progress UK Super User	INV_NAVIGATE	AZN_PR_INVENTORY
7	ABOASE	Payables Progress UK Healthcare	Progress UK Accounts Payable Menu (OPSFI)	AZN_PR_PAYABLES
8	ABOASE	Purchasing Progress UK Healthcare	Purchasing SuperUser GUI	AZN_PR_PROCUREMENT
9	ADB	General Ledger, Vision Banking, Manager	GL_SUPERUSER	AZN_PR_GL
10	ADB	Inventory, Vision Banking	INV_NAVIGATE	AZN_PR_ATO
11	ADB	Inventory, Vision Banking	INV_NAVIGATE	AZN_PR_INVENTORY
12	ADB	Payables, Vision Banking	AP_NAVIGATE_GUI12	AZN_PR_PAYABLES
13	ADB	Property Manager, Vision Banking	PN_NAVIGATE_CUSTOM	AZN_PR_PROPERTY_MANAGER
14	ADB	Purchasing, Vision Banking	Purchasing SuperUser GUI	AZN_PR_PROCUREMENT
15	AEHRMS	ERES Administrator	ERES Administrator	AZN_EDR_ERES_PROCESS

The easiest way to look at this data is by doing a pivot table as per the example below. By using a pivot table, you can see the specific AZN menus that remain available to use on each responsibility.

	A	B	C
1	Drop Report Filter Fields Here		
2			
3	Count of AZN_MENU_NAME		
4	RESPONSIBILITY_NAME ▼	AZN_MENU_NAME ▼	Total
5	⊟ Accounting Engine General Ledger Supervisor	AZN_PR_GL	1
6	Accounting Engine General Ledger Supervisor Total		1
7	⊟ Application Developer	AZN_MAIN	62
8	Application Developer Total		62
9	⊟ Application Developer, Vision Brazil	AZN_MAIN	1
10	Application Developer, Vision Brazil Total		1
11	⊟ Application Developer, US Federal	AZN_MAIN	1
12	Application Developer, US Federal Total		1
13	⊟ Applications Administration	AZN_MAIN	5
14	Applications Administration Total		5
15	⊟ AU General Ledger Super User	AZN_PR_GL	3
16	AU General Ledger Super User Total		3
17	⊟ AX General Ledger User MRC	AZN_PR_GL	1
18	AX General Ledger User MRC Total		1
19	⊟ AX Receivables User MRC	AZN_PR_RECEIVABLES	1

I do not recommend using AZN menus at all. Therefore, the pivot table provides you a list of responsibilities that need to have the AZN menu removed and the specific AZN menu that is causing the issue.

Following is a table providing detail of AZN menus and where they are contained as of the writing of this book:

Responsibility	USER_MENU_NAME	AZN_MENU_NAME
Applications Administration, System Administration Functions	System Administration Functions	AZN_MAIN, AZN_CASH_FORECASTIN G, AZN_EXPENSE_CYCLE, AZN_PJM_PRJ_DEF, AZN_PR_ASSET,

Responsibility	USER_MENU_NAME	AZN_MENU_NAME
		AZN_PR_ATO, AZN_PR_CLASSIFY_TO_C OUNT, AZN_PR_GL, AZN_PR_INTERNAL_REQ UISITION, AZN_PR_INVENTORY, AZN_PR_ORDER_FULFILL MENT, AZN_PR_PAYABLES, AZN_PR_PHYSICAL_INVE NTORY, AZN_PR_PROCUREMENT , AZN_PR_RECEIVABLES, AZN_REVENUE_CYCLE
Payables Manager	AP_NAVIGATE_GUI12	AZN_PR_PAYABLES
Receivables Manager	AR_NAVIGATE_GUI	AZN_PR_RECEIVABLES
ERES Security Administrator	ERES Administrator	AZN_EDR_ERES_PROCES S
Application Developer	Navigator Menu - Application Developer GUI	AZN_MAIN
Global Consolidation System Super User, Global Consolidation System User	GL_GCS_SU_MAIN	AZN_PR_GL
Global Intercompany System User	GL_GIS_SUPERUSER	AZN_PR_GL
General Ledger CENTRA User, General Ledger Controller, General Ledger Super User	GL_SUPERUSER	AZN_PR_GL
General Ledger Supervisor	GL_SUPERVISOR	AZN_PR_GL
Formulator	GMD_FORMULAS	AZN_PR_GMD

Responsibility	USER_MENU_NAME	AZN_MENU_NAME
Process Engineer, Formulation Chemist	GMD_RECIPES	AZN_PR_GMD
Inventory	INV_NAVIGATE	AZN_PR_ATO, AZN_PR_INVENTORY
OPM Product Development,	Application Navigator Menu Product Development	AZN_PR_GMD
Purchasing Super User	Purchasing SuperUser GUI	AZN_PR_PROCUREMENT

You have two options for remediating this risk:

1. The easiest option would be to apply a menu exclusion at the responsibility level. This would remove access to the AZN menu for users to which the responsibility is assigned.
2. The second option would be to redevelop responsibilities that are using the menus that contain AZN menus by developing a custom menu without the AZN menu.

See more on the risks related to AZN menus on our You Tube channel. See www.erpra.net for a link to our You Tube channel.

See Observation, Risk, and Recommendations in Chapter 10: OV-8 AZN menus.

Query 3: SQL Statement: Users with AZN Menus

```
SELECT u.user_name
,    u.description
,    u.start_date          user_start_date
,    u.end_date            user_end_date
,    a.application_name
,    a.application_short_name
,    r.responsibility_name
,    r.responsibility_key
,    r.responsibility_id
,    r.start_date          resp_start_date
,    r.end_date            resp_end_date
,    rg.start_date         assignment_start_date
,    rg.expiration_date     assignment_end_date
,    m.menu_name
,    m.user_menu_name
,    azn_m.menu_name        azn_menu_name
```

```sql
,    (    SELECT COUNT(*)
          FROM  apps.fnd_menu_entries    me1
          ,     apps.fnd_menus           m1
          WHERE me1.menu_id = r.menu_id
          AND   m1.menu_id = me1.sub_menu_id
          AND   m1.menu_name like 'AZN%') azn_menu_count
FROM  (
     SELECT wur.user_name
     ,      wur.role_orig_system_id
     ,      (    SELECT application_id
                 FROM apps.fnd_application
                 WHERE application_short_name =
                      REPLACE(SUBSTR( wur.role_name
                      ,     INSTR(wur.role_name, '|', 1, 1)+1
                      ,     (INSTR(wur.role_name, '|', 1, 2)-INSTR(wur.role_name,
'|', 1, 1)-1))
                      ,     '%col', ':')) resp_appl_id
     ,      wur.start_date
     ,      wur.expiration_date
     FROM   apps.wf_local_user_roles     wur
     WHERE  wur.role_orig_system = 'FND_RESP'
     AND    NOT wur.role_name LIKE 'FND_RESP|%|ANY'
     AND    wur.partition_id = 2
     AND    (((wur.start_date is NULL) OR (TRUNC(SYSDATE) >=
TRUNC(wur.start_date)))
     AND    ((wur.expiration_date IS NULL) OR (TRUNC(SYSDATE) <
trunc(wur.expiration_date)))
     AND    ((wur.user_start_date IS NULL) OR (TRUNC(SYSDATE) >=
trunc(wur.user_start_date)))
     AND    ((wur.user_end_date IS NULL) OR (TRUNC(SYSDATE) <
trunc(wur.user_end_date)))
     AND    ((wur.role_start_date IS NULL) OR (TRUNC(SYSDATE) >=
TRUNC(wur.role_start_date)))
     AND    ((wur.role_end_date IS NULL) OR (TRUNC(SYSDATE) <
trunc(wur.role_end_date)))))) rg
     ,      apps.fnd_user               u
     ,      apps.fnd_responsibility_vl    r
     ,      apps.fnd_application_vl       a
     ,      apps.fnd_menus_vl            m
     ,      apps.fnd_menu_entries    azn_me
     ,      apps.fnd_menus           azn_m
WHERE  u.user_name = rg.user_name
AND    r.responsibility_id = rg.role_orig_system_id
AND    r.application_id = rg.resp_appl_id
AND    a.application_id = r.application_id
AND    m.menu_id = r.menu_id
AND    azn_me.menu_id = r.menu_id
AND    azn_m.menu_id = azn_me.sub_menu_id
AND    azn_m.menu_name like 'AZN%'
AND EXISTS ( SELECT 1
          FROM apps.fnd_menu_entries    me1
          ,    apps.fnd_menus           m1
          WHERE me1.menu_id = r.menu_id
          AND   m1.menu_id = me1.sub_menu_id
          AND   m1.menu_name like 'AZN%')
```

ORDER BY 1,5,7,16

Chapter 31: Query 4: Generic Users

Purpose of the Query

This query returns the generic users seeded by Oracle still that remain active. This query supports audit test OV-4.

Evaluation of results
Sample data from Query 4: Generic Users

	A	C	D	E	F
1	USER_NAME	EMAIL_ADDRESS	START_DATE	EMPLOYEE_ID	PASSWORD_LIFESPAN_DAYS
2	AME_INVALID_APPROVER		01-JUL-04		
3	APPSMGR		01-JAN-51		
4	ASADMIN		08-JAN-09		
5	ASGADM		05-OCT-00		
6	AUTOINSTALL		01-JAN-51		
7	GUEST		27-NOV-96		5000
8	IEXADMIN		28-SEP-99		
9	INDUSTRY DATA		11-AUG-06		
10	IRC_EMP_GUEST		25-FEB-02		
11	IRC_EXT_GUEST		25-FEB-02		
12	MFG	jsmith	01-JAN-96	57	
13	MOBADM		27-AUG-04		
14	MOBDEV		27-AUG-04		
15	MOBILEADM		18-JUL-02		
16	OP_CUST_CARE_ADMIN		27-DEC-99		
17	OP_SYSADMIN		27-DEC-99		
18	ORACLE12.0.0		11-AUG-06		
19	ORACLE12.1.0		06-OCT-08		
20	ORACLE12.2.0		06-OCT-08		
21	ORACLE12.3.0		06-OCT-08		
22	ORACLE12.4.0		06-OCT-08		
23	ORACLE12.5.0		06-OCT-08		
24	ORACLE12.6.0		06-OCT-08		
25	ORACLE12.7.0		06-OCT-08		
26	ORACLE12.8.0		06-OCT-08		
27	ORACLE12.9.0		06-OCT-08		
28	SYSADMIN		01-JAN-51		
29	WIZARD	nobody@localhost	01-JAN-51		
30	XML_USER		11-JUN-03		

If one or more users are returned in the query it would indicate generic seeded users (provided by Oracle in the install of the applications or subsequent patches) are still active. You should compare those that are still active versus Oracle's recommendation in MOS Note 403537.1. Following is an excerpt as of the writing of this book:

CHANGE PASSWORDS FOR SEEDED APPLICATION USER ACCOUNTS

Oracle ships seeded user accounts with default passwords. Change the default passwords immediately. Depending on product usage, some seeded accounts may or may not be disabled. You disable an application user account by setting the END_DATE for the account.

- Do not disable the GUEST user account
- Do not disable the SYSADMIN user account until you have created other accounts with similar privilege

Note that we ship a script fnddefpw.sql, if you run this script as APPS it will list the seeded accounts that still have the default password.

In the table an 'x' in the EndDT column means the account ship end-dated.

In the table an 'x' in the NoPwd column indicates that the account ships with an "impossible password", this means that the password column in FND_USER contains a clear text string that is never a valid encrypted or hashed password. Thus it is not possible to login as this user, - unless you change the password!

In order to validate that there are no unintended consequences of disabling such accounts, the organization should thoroughly test the disabling of these accounts in a non-production environment. Following are the recommendation as of the writing of this book:

Account	Product / Purpose	Change	Disable	NoPwd	EndDT
AME_INVALID_APPROVER	AME WF migration 11.5.9 to 11.5.10	Y	Y		
ANONYMOUS	FND/AOL – Anonymous for non-logged users	Y	Y		x
APPSMGR	Routine maintenance via concurrent requests	N	Y	x	x
ASADMIN	Application Server Administrator	N	Y	x	x
ASGADM	Mobile gateway related products	Y	Y[a]		
ASGUEST	Sales Application guest user	Y	Y[b]		
AUTOINSTALL	AD	Y	Y		
CONCURRENT MANAGER	FND/AOL: Concurrent Manager	Y	Y		x
FEEDER SYSTEM	AD – Supports data from feeder system	Y	Y		x
GUEST	Guest application user	Y	N		
IBE_ADMIN	iStore Admin user	Y	Y[c]		
IBE_GUEST	iStore Guest user	Y	Y[c]		
IBEGUEST	iStore Guest user	Y	Y[c]		
IEXADMIN	Internet Expenses Admin	Y	Y		
INDUSTRY DATA		N	Y	x	
INITIAL SETUP	AD	Y	Y		x
IRC_EMP_GUEST	iRecruitment Employee Guest Login	Y	Y		
IRC_EXT_GUEST	iRecruitment External Guest Login	Y	Y		
MOBILEADM	Mobile Applications Admin	Y	Y		
MOBILEDEV	Mobile Applications Development	Y	Y		
OP_CUST_CARE_ADMIN	Customer Care Admin for Oracle Provisioning	Y	Y		
OP_SYSADMIN	OP (Process Manufacturing) Admin User	Y	Y		
ORACLE12.[0-9].0	Owner for release specific seed data	N	N	x	
PORTAL30	Desupported Portal 3.0.x Account	Y	Y		
PORTAL30_SSO	Desupported Portal 3.0.x Account	Y	Y		
STANDALONE BATCH PROCESS	FND/AOL	Y	Y		
SYSADMIN	Application Systems Admin	Y	N		
WIZARD	AD – Application Implementation Wizard	Y	Y		
XML_USER	Gateway	Y	Y		

a. Required for Mobile Sales, Service, and Mobile Core Gateway components.
b. Required for Sales Application.
c. Required for iStore.

See Observation, Risk, and Recommendations in Chapter 6: OV-4 Generic Users - Vendor.

Query 4: SQL Statement: Generic Users

```
SELECT a.user_name,
    a.description,
    a.email_address email_address,
    a.start_date,
    a.employee_id,
    a.password_lifespan_days
FROM   fnd_user a
WHERE  a.end_date IS NULL
    AND a.user_name IN
('GUEST','AME_INVALID_APPROVER','ANONYMOUS','APPSMGR',
'ASGADM','ASGUEST','AUTOINSTALL','BOL-OPS',                'BOL-
SETUP','BOL-SUPPORT','CONCURRENT MANAGER','FEEDER SYSTEM',
'IBE_ADMIN','IBE_GUEST','IBEGUEST','IEXADMIN',
'INITIAL_SETUP','IRC_EMP_GUEST','IRC_EXT_GUEST','MOBILEADM','MOBADM','
MOBDEV','OP_CUST_CARE_ADMIN','OP_SYSADMIN',
'PORTAL30','PORTAL30_SSO','STANDALONE BATCH PROCESS','SYSADMIN',
'WIZARD','XML_USER', 'ORACLE12.0.0', 'ORACLE12.1.0', 'ORACLE12.2.0',
'ORACLE12.3.0', 'ORACLE12.4.0', 'ORACLE12.5.0', 'ORACLE12.6.0',
'ORACLE12.7.0', 'ORACLE12.8.0', 'ORACLE12.9.0', 'INDUSTRY DATA', 'ASADMIN',
'OA_IMPLEMENTER', 'PASYSADMIN', 'MFG', 'PRESETUP', 'SETUP',
'CONVERSION', 'CONVERSIONS')
```

Chapter 32: Query 5: Profile Options

Purpose of the Query

Query for all profile options set – will be used to review various critical profile options such as Utilities:Diagnostics and those related password controls. This query supports audit test OV-10, OV-11, and OV-17.

Evaluation of results

Oracle provides over 8,000 profile options which have a wide variety of uses. Following are some examples:

User Profile Option Name	Purpose / Comments
Signon Password Length	This determines the minimum password length for the Application Users. This setting is something that is typically set at the Site level and, therefore, would apply to all Users throughout the system. However, it can also be set different for certain Users by applying it at the "User" level.
Utilities: Diagnostics	When enabled this allows users to see and change certain information that is not accessible through the normal user interface. This 'back door' access is only available through Forms, not HTML pages. Because this would allow a user to changes data fields such as "IDs" I don't recommend allowing anyone to have access this in Prod. See a video on this topic at our YouTube channel which can be accessed through a link at www.erpra.net.

User Profile Option Name	Purpose / Comments
GL: Journal Review Required	This profile determines whether or not a journal entry that is generated from a Mass Allocation (aka Allocation Formulas) is subject to the Journal Approval Workflow. In essence, this is part of the configurations related to the Journal Approval Workflow. Therefore, the setting of this profile option should support the intent of the control design. This is a journal entry I would expect would be set at the Site level. However, Oracle allows this to be set at the User level both through the System Profile Values form and the User Profile Values form.

I provided three examples of profile options with very different risks and recommended settings to give you an idea of the complexities related to auditing profile options. Evaluating every profile option that is set should not be the goal as it would take too long the scope of most audits. My recommendation is to start with 20 or 30 of the higher risk profile options we have provided as part of the Profile Options Risk Assessment template which you can access via the Book Resources page at www.erpra.net. Start with those listed with a Risk Rating of 'High'. Also, if you identify any of the profile options that could impact application controls (also provided in the Profile Options Risk Assessment file) you should evaluate those also.

Let's now look at some sample data.

Sample data from Query 5: Profile Options

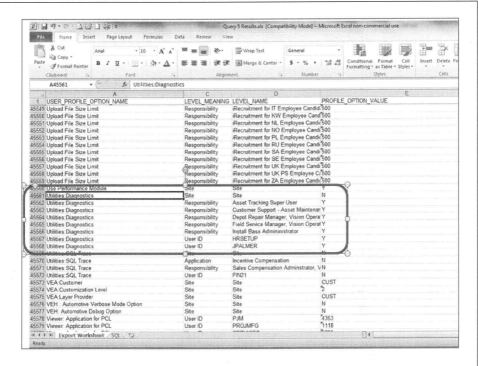

In this sample data, we look at one of our favorite issues which was given as an example above. We have the 'Utilities: Diagnostics' profile option set the Site level to 'N' which is what we recommend. However, it is overridden at the Responsibility and User levels. Even though it is set to 'N' at the Site level, if a user is using the Asset Tracking Super User, Customer Support – Asset Maintenance, Depot Repair – Vision Operations, Field Service Manager, Vision Operations, or Install Base Administrator responsibilities, he/she is allowed to access the Diagnostics menu because the profile option is set to 'Y' at those levels. Users logged in a HRSETUP and JPALMER user accounts can also access the Diagnostics menu in ANY responsibility they are using.

So, when auditing profile options, you need to ask a few questions:

- What are the risks associated with the profile option? What does it enable or prevent?
- At which level (Site, Application, Responsibility, or User) can it be set? Not all profile options can be set at all levels.
- At which level should it be set? Just because it CAN be set at a certain level, should it be? The Utilities: Diagnostics is a good example where it can be set at the Site, Application,

Responsibility, and User levels, but we would recommend not setting to 'Y" at any level. It should only be set to 'N' at the Site level (at least in Production).

- Should the profile option be subject to your organization's change management process?
- Have the profile options that have been set been properly approved? The key is 'properly' approved. For example - can a business analyst approve a change or does the change need to be approved by an IT Compliance Manager or perhaps once set, a change should never be approved as would be the case in the 'Utilities: Diagnostics' profile option?

These questions form the basis of the Profile Options Risk Assessment that is necessary to perform and provide to the security administrators that are responsible for analyzing the appropriateness of requests to change profile options.

As a reminder, following is the format of the Profile Options Risk Assessment template and the recommendations related to the Utilities: Diagnostics profile option.

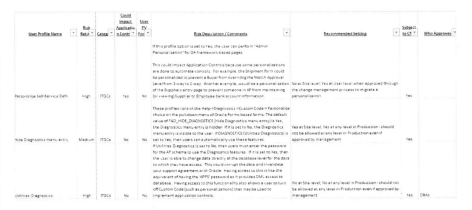

For the latest template related to the Profile Options Risk Assessment see the Book Resources page at www.erpra.net, or send us an email at admin@erpra.net. Please also sent us an email if you identify one or more profile options that you believe should be added to the Profile Options Risk Assessment or you would suggest a change to one we already have documented.

Query 5: Profile Options

```
SELECT  ot.user_profile_option_name
, TO_CHAR(v.level_id) level_id
, DECODE(v.level_id
    ,10001,'Site'
    , 10002,'Application'
    , 10003,'Responsibility'
    , 10004,'User ID'
    , v.level_id)
  level_meaning
, DECODE(v.level_id
    ,10001,'Site'
    , 10002,apl.application_name
    , 10003,frt.responsibility_name
    , 10004,u.user_name
    , v.level_id)
  level_name
, v.profile_option_value
, o.profile_option_name
, v.creation_date value_creation_date
, v.created_by value_created_by
, v.last_update_date value_last_updated_date
, v.last_updated_by value_last_updated_by
FROM   applsys.fnd_profile_options_tl ot
, applsys.fnd_profile_options o
, applsys.fnd_profile_option_values v
, applsys.fnd_responsibility_tl frt
, apps.fnd_application_vl apl
, fnd_user u
WHERE  v.level_value      = frt.responsibility_id (+)
  AND v.profile_option_id = o.profile_option_id
  AND o.profile_option_name = ot.profile_option_name
  AND ot.language         = 'US'
  AND NVL(frt.language,'US') = 'US'
  AND v.level_value       = apl.application_id (+)
    AND u.user_id (+) = v.level_value
ORDER BY ot.user_profile_option_name
, v.level_id
, DECODE(v.level_id
    ,10001,'Site'
    , 10002,'Application'
    , 10003,frt.responsibility_name
    , 10004,u.user_name
    , v.level_id);
```

Chapter 33: Query 6: Stale Users

Purpose of the Query

Returns users that haven't logged in the past 60 days; users may need to be end-dated. This could be used to identify terminated users that have not be end-dated or just accounts that aren't being used. This query supports audit test OV-6.

This query identifies User accounts that haven't signed into the applications in the past 60 days. This is what we refer to as 'stale' users. This may be an indication that the account needs to be disabled altogether.

However, if your organization uses certain applications such as Employee Self-Service or iRecruitment, the identification of users that haven't logged into the applications in the past 60 days would not necessarily indicate the account is stale.

In this query, we identify the responsibilities that are assigned to the user. So, if the user only has a responsibility that is rarely used, it may be appropriate to leave the account active.

One of the benefits of disabling stale users may be savings on your Oracle software licenses if the applications are based on named users.

Evaluation of results
Sample data from Query 6: Stale Users

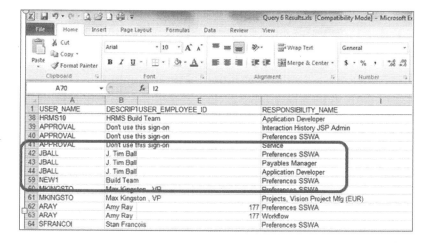

In these query results, we have two different results. For JBALL, this User has access to the Payables Manager and Application Developer Responsibilities. If he/she isn't using this login it should be disabled immediately due to the high risk nature of these responsibilities as well as the possible impact on licensing. For NEW1, the only assigned responsibility is Preferences SSWA which is a responsibility sometimes assigned to users that allows them to maintain their preferences such as the Number Format and Time Zone. Because this is low risk access and likely doesn't impact license issues, this may not be worth pursuing unless you believe it could have an impact on license costs.

There are a couple of approaches you could take once you identify Users that are stale or may be stale.

1. End-date, force users to re-justify their login, run script to change password and force to use self-service password reset capability.

2. Contact the user(s) and/or their manager to ask them if their access is needed.

Query 6: Stale Users

```
SELECT  u.user_name
   ,    u.description
   ,    u.start_date              user_start_date
   ,    u.end_date               user_end_date
   ,    u. employee_id           user_employee_id
   ,    u. password_lifespan_days          user_password_expiration_days
   ,    a.application_name
   ,    a.application_short_name
   ,    r.responsibility_name
   ,    r.responsibility_key
   ,    r.responsibility_id
   ,    r.start_date              resp_start_date
   ,    r.end_date               resp_end_date
   ,    rg.start_date            assignment_start_date
   ,    rg.expiration_date         assignment_end_date
FROM  (
     SELECT  wur.user_name
        ,    wur.role_orig_system_id
        ,    (    SELECT application_id
                FROM apps.fnd_application
                WHERE application_short_name =
                    REPLACE(SUBSTR( wur.role_name
                        ,    INSTR(wur.role_name, '|', 1, 1)+1
                        ,    (INSTR(wur.role_name, '|', 1, 2)-INSTR(wur.role_name,
'|', 1, 1)-1))
                        ,    '%col', ':')) resp_appl_id
        ,    wur.start_date
        ,    wur.expiration_date
     FROM   apps.wf_local_user_roles     wur
     WHERE  wur.role_orig_system = 'FND_RESP'
     AND    NOT wur.role_name LIKE 'FND_RESP|%|ANY'
     AND    wur.partition_id = 2
     AND    (((wur.start_date is NULL) OR (TRUNC(SYSDATE) >=
TRUNC(wur.start_date)))
     AND    ((wur.expiration_date IS NULL) OR (TRUNC(SYSDATE) <
trunc(wur.expiration_date)))
     AND    ((wur.user_start_date IS NULL) OR (TRUNC(SYSDATE) >=
trunc(wur.user_start_date)))
     AND    ((wur.user_end_date IS NULL) OR (TRUNC(SYSDATE) <
trunc(wur.user_end_date)))
     AND    ((wur.role_start_date IS NULL) OR (TRUNC(SYSDATE) >=
TRUNC(wur.role_start_date)))
     AND    ((wur.role_end_date IS NULL) OR (TRUNC(SYSDATE) <
trunc(wur.role_end_date))))) rg
        ,    apps.fnd_user u
        ,    apps.fnd_responsibility_vl r
        ,    apps.fnd_application_vl a
WHERE  u.user_name = rg.user_name
AND    r.responsibility_id = rg.role_orig_system_id
AND    r.application_id = rg.resp_appl_id
```

```
AND    a.application_id = r.application_id
and    (a.last_logon_date < sysdate - 60
       or a.last_logon_date is null and a.start_date < sysdate - 15)
and    a.user_name not in ('GUEST')
order by a.last_logon_date ;
```

Here is a simpler version of the stale users if you don't want the responsibilities associated with each stale user:

```
Select  a.user_name, a.description, a.email_address EMAIL_ADDRESS,
a.start_date, a.last_logon_date, NVL(TO_CHAR(sysdate-
a.last_logon_date,'999,999'),' NEVER') days_ago, b.description CREATED_BY,
a.last_update_date, c.description LAST_UPDATED_BY
from    fnd_user a, fnd_user b, fnd_user c
where   a.created_by = b.user_id
AND    a.last_updated_by = c.user_id
and    a.end_date is null
and    (a.last_logon_date < sysdate - 60
       or a.last_logon_date is null and a.start_date < sysdate - 15)
and    a.user_name not in ('GUEST')
order by a.last_logon_date ;
```

Chapter 34: Query 7: Possible Terminated Application Users

Purpose of the Query

This query returns more results than necessary. I will work on refining the query in a future release. This query returns users terminated in HR, but with User account still active. This query supports audit test OV-7.

This query identifies Users that are possibly terminated employees who would need to have their User account terminated. This query is only effective if the HR system is being used. If the HR system is not being used this query may still be valuable if the termination data is being interfaced from the HR system in a timely manner.

Evaluation of results
Sample data from Query 7: Possible Terminated Application Users

	A	H	I
1	USER_NAME	USER_PERSON_TYPE	ACTUAL_TERMINATION_DATE
1217	ATAYLOR	Employee	
1218	ISUPPORTADMIN	Employee	
1219	BTAYLOR	Employee	
1220	MTAYLOR	Employee	
1221	PATAYLOR	Employee	
1222	PTAYLOR	Employee	
1223	EBUSINESS	Employee	
1224	COMMS_ISTORE	Employee	
1225	SXTAYLOR	Employee	
1226	SATAYLOR	Employee	
1227	JTAYLOR	Employee	
1228	NLHRTRAIN	Employee	
1229	LTENDON	Ex-employee	29-MAY-10
1230	STHANGAWELU	Employee	

In these query results, you are looking for the presence of data in the ACTUAL_TERMINATION_DATE column. Often you will also see the USER_PERSON_TYPE field as 'Ex-employee' as is the case in the above example. However, sometimes the data may still show as 'Employee, 'Employee and Applicant' or another status. We recommend whenever there is a value in the ACTUAL_TERMINATION_DATE column that you follow up to determine why the User account (in the example above - 'LTENDON') is still active. This could be an indication of a flaw in the terminations process.

Query 7: Possible Terminated Application Users

```
select fu.user_name,
    fu.description,
    papf.full_name,
    papf.person_id,
    fu.last_logon_date,
    fu.start_date,
    fu.password_lifespan_days,
    ppt.user_person_type,
    ser.actual_termination_date
from  applsys.fnd_user fu,
 hr.per_all_people_f papf,
 hr.per_person_types ppt,
 hr.per_periods_of_service ser
where fu.employee_id = papf.person_id
 and papf.person_type_id = ppt.person_type_id
 and sysdate between papf.effective_start_date and effective_end_date
 and fu.end_date is null
 and fu.created_by <> 1
 and papf.person_id = ser.person_id
 and ser.date_start in
     (select max(date_start)
        from hr.per_periods_of_service
        where person_id = papf.person_id)
order by papf.full_name
```

Chapter 35: Query 8: Possible generic users

Purpose of the Query

If a User account does not have an employee associated with it, it could be a generic user. This query supports audit test OV-5.

This query returns a list of Users without an employee assigned to it. This is normally the result of one of the following reasons:
1. Seeded Oracle Users
2. A custom generic User
3. Contractors where there is not an employee record
4. Temporary employees where there is not an employee record
5. Your organization does not associate an employee with each Oracle User account
6. Your organization uses an application such as iRecruitment that does not associate a User with an employee record.

Evaluation of results
Sample data from Query 8: Possible generic users

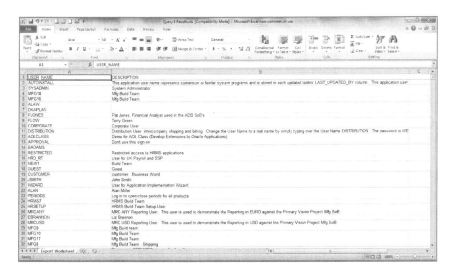

In these query results, you may recognize some of the user accounts from query 4 above. Typically, the seeded generic users (provided by Oracle as part of the install or from a patch) do not have an employee associated them. In this query, you are looking for other accounts that aren't seeded. These may be the result of a custom generic user being set up. Of the data above, you can see many examples of users that are not seeded – MFG18, MFG16, ALAW, DKAPLAN,

PJONES, and many more. You should discuss these with the security administration team. Ask if a risk assessment for each has been performed and approved by management. Compare the purpose of these to your policy related to the use (or prohibition of use) of generic logics.

If one or more of these need to remain active and have a 'valid' purpose, you may want to review the responsibilities assigned to the user account which can be done by looking at the data in Query 2 above.

Here are some possible recommendations based on the results of the query:

1. Seeded Oracle users – see recommendations in Query 4 related to Oracle seeded users.

2. Custom generic users – some custom generic users are ok and some are not. Most organizations have a policy that says generic users are not allowed, but most systems have them. If there are generic users present in your Oracle applications, a risk assessment should be documented and management should sign off on the risks. See the chapter in my book Oracle E-Business Suite Controls: Application Security Best Practices or upcoming book Oracle E-Business Suite Controls: Foundation Principles on best practices related to Users for more on this topic.

   In summary of those recommendations, generic users should have their usage monitored and their assigned roles and responsibilities very limited. We also recommend the 'owners' of those accounts justify their usage by logging their access and someone independent of the 'owner' review a system report such as the Signon Audit Login report compared to the 'log' of the activity to make sure the 'owner(s)' is compliant with the policy.

   In many cases, we see excessive access to responsibilities with update-type access that can be done through the generic user that would not be acceptable to management.

   One type of 'acceptable' generic user is a job scheduling user.

3. Contractors where there is no employee record associated with the User account – in some organizations this is acceptable because the organization does not require an 'employee' record be created for the contractor. In some organizations, an 'employee' record is required to be created which would mean the absence of an employee record would be a finding. Whether or not an employee record is required to be associate d with a User account, contractor's accounts should be regularly re-confirmed with the 'hiring' manager that the access is still needed. This is because contractor 'terminations' sometimes slip through the cracks since they don't always follow the same terminations process as employees.

4. Temporary employees – this is similar to the comments in '3' above related to contractors. A temporary employee may be treated more like an employee or a contractor. If your organization requires that a temporary employee be set up as an 'employee' in Oracle, then investigate why the User account is not associated with an employee.

5. Your organization does not associate an employee with an Oracle User account – this would be out of the ordinary as most organizations have one or more workflow processes that require the User account to have an employee record associated with it. This scenario should be investigated in more detail.

6. Your organization uses an application that creates User accounts (such as iRecruitment) that doesn't automatically create an associated employee record. Therefore, this may be 'normal' and not subject to further investigation.

The results of the query could also identify a combination of the above scenarios discussed as 1 – 6 above. Each record returned in this query should be investigated as to which scenario matches its situation and investigated until you are confident of the related risk, if any, with each User account.

Query 8: Possible Generic Users

Select user_name, description
From fnd_user
Where EMPLOYEE_ID is null and end_date is null

Chapter 36: Query 9: Users where count of Employee ID is greater than 1

Purpose of the Query

This query would identify employees assigned to more than one User. This query supports audit test OV-25.

The presence of data returned in this query is unusual and requires investigation. This may indicate duplicate users or ghost accounts (users not associated with a valid employee). Even though I have never run across a scenario where this is the case, some functionality in the application may not work properly if there an employee is assigned to more than one user.

Evaluation of results

Sample data from Query 9: Users where count of Employee ID is greater than 1

	A	B	C	D
1	FULL_NAME	EMPLOYEE_NUMBER	USER_NAME	DESCRIPTION
2	Abbott, Ms. Rhonda	205	4RABBOTT	
3	Abbott, Ms. Rhonda	205	RABBOTT	
4	Aizawa Haruhiko / Aizawa_kanji Haruhiko_kanji	JPC00006	HAIZAWA_JPC	Japan Corp Purchasing
5	Aizawa Haruhiko / Aizawa_kanji Haruhiko_kanji	JPC00008	JAPANCORP	JAPANCORP USER
6	Banks, Mrs. Susan	1872	OPR1	
7	Banks, Mrs. Susan	1872	INT_AUD1	Internal Auditor
8	Barton, Jeffrey M	509	EBUSINESS MANUFACTURING	Complete EBusiness user for the Vision Operations Organization
9	Barton, Jeffrey M	509	EBUSINESS-MFG	Complete EBusiness Suite user for Vision Operations Set of Books
10	Benson, Ms. Peggy Kaye	17	PBENSON	Peggy Benson
11	Benson, Ms. Peggy Kaye	17	BENSO17	
12	Benson, Peggy Kaye	17	PBENSON	Peggy Benson
13	Benson, Peggy Kaye	17	PBENSON	Peggy Benson
14	Benson, Peggy Kaye	17	BENSO17	
15	Benson, Peggy Kaye	17	BENSO17	
16	Brady, Ms. Kathy	925	BANKING	Vision Banking User
17	Brady, Ms. Kathy	925	ADB	

In these query results, you should inquire about each record. Why does Ms. Rhonda Abbott have two user accounts – 4RABBOTT and RABBOTT? What does Mr. Todd Evans have two user accounts – LEAD_AUD and ADMIN1?

I recommend asking why there is multiple User accounts related to an employee. There are sometimes valid reasons where this is the case.

However, extra accounts should typically be disabled. If the explanation provided by your organization doesn't make sense, send us an email at admin@erpra.net and we would be happy to respond with our thoughts.

Query 9: Users where count of Employee ID is greater than 1

```
SELECT  p.full_name
,       p.employee_number
,       u.user_name
,       u.description
FROM    fnd_user  u
,       per_all_people_f p
WHERE   u.employee_id IN(
        SELECT  employee_id
        FROM    fnd_user
        WHERE   employee_id IS NOT NULL
        GROUP BY employee_id
        HAVING COUNT(*) > 1  )
AND     p.person_id = u.employee_id
ORDER BY 1,2
```

Chapter 37: Query 10: Request Groups Definitions

Purpose of the Query

Identify which request groups have access to sensitive reports and programs. These queries supports audit test OV-14.

This query returns the results of all data in request groups. There are four sub-queries as follows:

A. The first one returns "Programs" assigned to each Request Group
B. The second one returns the details "Request Sets" assigned to each Request Group
C. The third one returns the details of "Application" types assigned to each Request Group
D. The fourth query returns the details of all Request Sets so you can identify which programs are associated with the Request Sets that are assigned to each Request Group.

In total, these four queries give you the information you need to look for which Request Groups / Responsibilities / Users that have access to sensitive reports and high risk Concurrent Programs (examples include those that process data, interface programs, programs that purge or archive data, and programs that decrypt encrypted data).

The assessment could be vary significantly depending on the number of hours you have for your assessment. The starting point would be to develop a list of what you consider to be a high risk Concurrent Program. If management hasn't developed such a list, that would be a good first finding.

Example of list of high risk concurrent programs

Module	Report Name	Related risk	Comments
AP	Supplier Mailing Labels	Employee and supplier addresses	Report can include employee address information if they are set to receive payments from AP to their home
AP	1099 Reports (various - 24+ reports)	Employee and supplier EINs (not normal to have employees) / Employee and supplier addresses and bank accounts	Report can include employee home address and bank information if they are set to receive payments from AP to their home
AP	Final Payment Register	Employee and supplier addresses	Report can include employee home address if they are set to receive payments from AP to their home
AP	Payment Register	Employee and supplier addresses	Report can include employee home address if they are set to receive payments from AP to their home
PO	New Vendor Letter Report	Employee and supplier addresses	Employee home address information can be obtained via this report with the parameter of Type = Employee
AR	Customer Listing - Detailed	Customer names and addresses	This report gives a complete detailed listing of all your customers, their addresses, and contacts information. It would be valuable information in the hands of your competitors. This report also gives you access to sensitive customer bank information if you enter Bank information with a type of Customer.
AR	Customer Listing - Summary	Customer names and addresses	Summarized version of the above
AR	Assign Customer Credit Classification Program		This program allows a user to update update the credit classification for all customers who were already assigned to a profile.
PO	Pay On Receipt Autoinvoice	Allows autoinvoicing for received goods/services	This program automatically creates electron invoices that are matched to the receipt / PO and processed without having to enter an AP invoice.
PO	Pay on Receipt Autoinvoice Program	Matching of invoices to purchase orders	Automatically creates invoices in Payables and match them to corresponding purchase orders where Pay on Receipt functionality is enabled. Essentially this means the Receipt of Goods related to a PO generates an invoice and doesn't require an invoice to be entered in order for it to be paid.
Workflow	Purge Obsolete Workflow Runtime Data	Automated Controls / Workflow History Retention	This is typically a scheduled job that purges workflow history information, including workflow approvals and notifications. If this information is purged workflow history may not be available for testing by internal and external auditors.
Overall	Decrypt Credit Card Data	Allows for decryption of credit card data	Should never be allowed to be assigned to a request group in ANY environment including production and non-production environments
Overall	Decrypt External Bank Account Data	Allows for decryption of supplier bank account data	Should never be allowed to be assigned to a request group in ANY environment including production and non-production environments
Overall	Decrypt Transaction Extension Data	Allows for decryption of credit card data	Should never be allowed to be assigned to a request group in ANY environment including production and non-production environments

The latest template documenting high risk concurrent programs can be found on our Book Resources page at www.erpra.net.

The extent of your testing would depend on how confident you are of the quality of the design of request groups as well as the change management process since their initial design.

Consider these responses to these questions as part of the Internal Controls Questionnaire:

- Did you document which concurrent programs are high risk? Think about interface programs, conversion programs, and reports with access to sensitive data (both custom and seeded)?
- Was it clearly documented what constituted sensitive data and high risk concurrent programs from the beginning of the project? As custom programs were developed, was a list maintained as per the above example?
- Were those that were responsible for approving custom request groups or use of seeded request groups in responsibilities aware of which reports contained sensitive data?

- Were those responsible for approving changes to request groups aware of the high risk concurrent programs including those that contain sensitive data?

If you have concerns about the thoroughness of the process based on these questions above, attempt to identify a couple of examples where one or more Responsibilities have access to Concurrent Programs that would not be appropriate.

One recurring issue I've seen is the use of a seeded (provided by Oracle) request group in the design of an Inquiry Responsibility. Look through Query 2 to identify one or more Responsibility with Inquiry in the name. Review the Request Group assigned to that Responsibility in Query 1. Then look at the Concurrent Programs assigned to that Request Group in Query 10a below. You may find these Request Groups being used in an Inquiry Responsibility:

Request Group Name	Module
All Reports (Purchasing)	Purchasing
All Reports (Assets)	Assets
All Reports (Payables)	Payables
All Reports (Cash Management)	Cash Management
All Reports (Manufacturing)	Various modules
All Reports (Quality)	Quality
GL Concurrent Program Group	General Ledger
Receivables All	Receivables
All Inclusive GUI	Inventory

Following are some examples of high risk concurrent programs in these Request Groups:

Request Group Name	Module	Concurrent Program
All Reports (Purchasing)	Purchasing	Purge Catalog interMedia Index Populate Endeca Metadata for iProcurement Rebuild Catalog interMedia Index Receiving Transaction Processor
All Reports (Assets)	Assets	Create Accounting – Assets Transfer Journal Entries to GL – Assets Mass Additions Create

Request Group Name	Module	Concurrent Program
All Reports (Payables)	Payables	Payables (Application) - provides access to ALL Concurrent Programs for the Payables module Payables Open Interface Purge MRC Setup - Payables Transactions Upgrade: Phase 1 Supplier Open Interface Import Supplier Sites Open Interface Import
All Reports (Cash Management)	Cash Management	Cash Management (Application) - provides access to ALL Concurrent Programs for the Cash Management module Subledger Accounting (Application) - provides access to ALL Concurrent Programs for the Subledger Accounting module
All Reports (Manufacturing)	Various modules	Purchasing (Application) Inventory (Application) Shop Floor Management (Application) Bills of Material (Application) Engineering (Application) Master Scheduling/MRP (Application) Capacity (Application) Work in Process (Application) The above provides full access to all Concurrent Programs for all these modules
All Reports (Quality)	Quality	Quality (Application) – provides access to ALL Concurrent Programs for the Quality module
GL Concurrent Program Group	General Ledger	Open Period Program - Delete Journal Import Data Translation Program - Revalue Balances Program - Automatic Posting Program - Delete Budget Organization Program - Maintain Budget Organization Program - Create Journals
Receivables All	Receivables	Autoinvoice Import Program Customer Interface Customer Merge Sales Tax Rate Interface Autoinvoice Master Program

Request Group Name	Module	Concurrent Program
		Generate key for fuzzy match
All Inclusive GUI	Inventory	Purge replenishment counts
		Transaction Purge
		Purge cycle count entries open interface
		Costgroup upgrade for closed periods

See below related to the Query 10c for more explanation of how the "Application" type assignments to Request Group work.

Evaluation of results

The four queries 10a, 10b, 10c, and 10d all work together. Taken as a whole, they identify what concurrent programs can be run by a particular responsibility. Let's first illustrate how they work together and then we will draw some conclusions. We are going to look at the same Request Group in all three examples below – that being the "All Reports" request group for the Payables module.

One thing to note about Request Groups is they are uniquely identified by a combination of the name and the module. You can have an "All Reports" request group in different modules as follows:

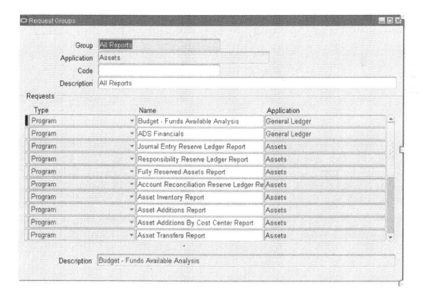

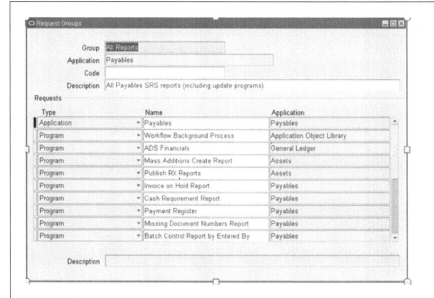

Sample data from Query 10a: Request Groups

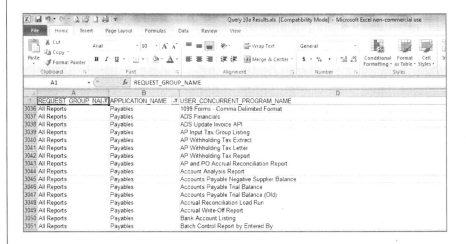

In these query results, you get a complete list of all concurrent programs that are assigned to a Request Group.

Sample 2 for Query 10a: Request Groups

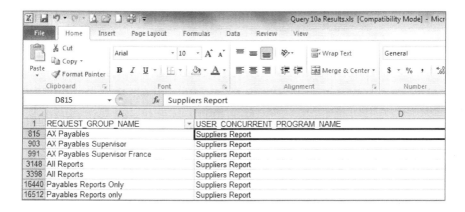

You can also use the Filter function in Excel to see which Request Groups have access to high risk reports. You can use this in conjunction with your list of high risk concurrent programs that you should be keeping in a spreadsheet such as this:

Sample data from Query 10b: Request Sets for Request Groups

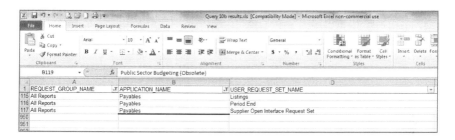

This is an example of the results of which Request Sets are included in the "All Reports" Request Group for the Payables module.

Sample data from Query 10c: Applications for Request Groups

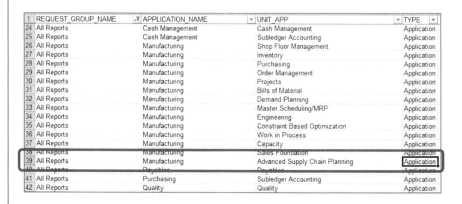

	REQUEST_GROUP_NAME	APPLICATION_NAME	UNIT_APP	TYPE
24	All Reports	Cash Management	Cash Management	Application
25	All Reports	Cash Management	Subledger Accounting	Application
26	All Reports	Manufacturing	Shop Floor Management	Application
27	All Reports	Manufacturing	Inventory	Application
28	All Reports	Manufacturing	Purchasing	Application
29	All Reports	Manufacturing	Order Management	Application
30	All Reports	Manufacturing	Projects	Application
31	All Reports	Manufacturing	Bills of Material	Application
32	All Reports	Manufacturing	Demand Planning	Application
33	All Reports	Manufacturing	Master Scheduling/MRP	Application
34	All Reports	Manufacturing	Engineering	Application
35	All Reports	Manufacturing	Constraint Based Optimization	Application
36	All Reports	Manufacturing	Work in Process	Application
37	All Reports	Manufacturing	Capacity	Application
38	All Reports	Manufacturing	Sales Foundation	Application
39	All Reports	Manufacturing	Advanced Supply Chain Planning	Application
40	All Reports	Payables	Payables	Application
41	All Reports	Purchasing	Subledger Accounting	Application
42	All Reports	Quality	Quality	Application

To help complete the picture of how Request groups work, let's look at how the All Reports / Payables request group looks in the application as shown following:

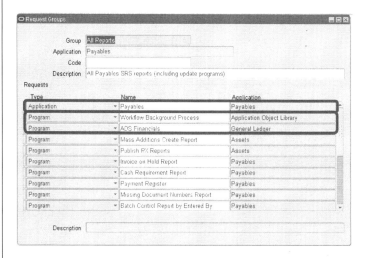

And scrolling down to the bottom, provides the rest of the information as follows:

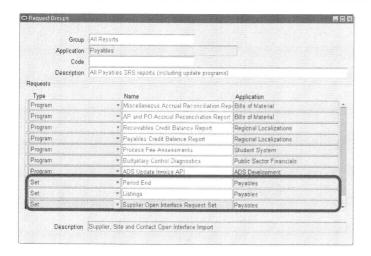

This request group has three things to take into consideration – it has some individual concurrent programs assigned to it such as "Workflow Background Process" and "ADS Financials", it has an Application associated with it – Payables and three Request Sets associated with it.

To illustrate how Request Sets work, following shows a screen shot of the Supplier Open Interface Request Set:

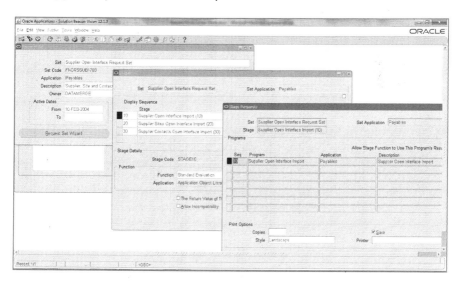

A request set is used to run a series of concurrent requests or concurrent requests that have dependencies on prior requests. In this illustration, we have three sequences. Each sequence can contain one or more concurrent programs. In the third screen shot, we have the detail of what concurrent programs can be run in the first sequence shown in screen shot 2 (Sequence 10). So, to understand what reports or programs can be run via a Request Set, we need to peel back each underlying sequence. It identifies the concurrent programs that can be run in a given Request Set, regardless of at what stage.

The third component of determining what concurrent programs can be run via the request group is determining if an 'Application' is associated with it. In our example, the fact that the Application 'Payables' is associated with it means it can run ALL concurrent programs that are identified with the Payables module. Let us illustrate how this work with an example.

First, we set up a simple Request Group with just two concurrent programs as follows:

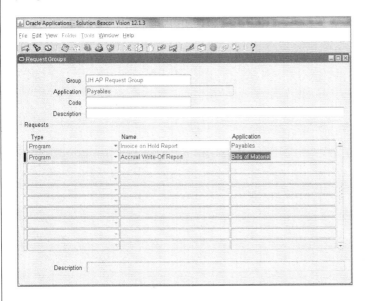

When we go into the Requests: Submit form, we see just the two concurrent programs that we have identified in the Request Group above.

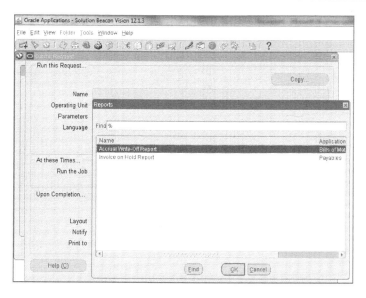

Next, we add a line to the Request Group to add the Application 'Payables' as follows:

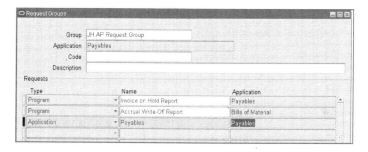

When we return to the Requests: Submit menu, we now see a whole bunch more concurrent programs that can be run. In fact, the count in the bottom left says we now have 167 different concurrent programs that we can run.

The addition of the Application 'Payables' to the Request Group has added 165 concurrent programs – essentially ALL available concurrent programs associated with the Payables module.

Conclusions related to Request Groups

Essentially what we are trying to evaluate is whether or not users have access to the concurrent programs and reports they need to do their job and do not have access to high risk concurrent programs or reports with sensitive data that are not appropriate for their job role. An evaluation should be done with existing Request Groups to determine that access is appropriate. A custom Request Group should also be designed and used for each role to avoid Upgrade Risk – the risk that a patch will add one or more concurrent programs to a Request Group that may not be appropriate for all the users.

Following are recommendations that typically are the result of this query:
1. Use custom request groups

2. Principle of least privilege Build each request group from the ground up

3. Review for access to sensitive request groups

4. Do not use "Applications" in Request Group design since they provide access to ALL requests related to a given application.

SQL Queries for this chapter

Query 10a: What Concurrent Programs are contained in each Request Group

```
-- The first one is for "Programs" only.
SELECT a.request_group_name, e.application_name, a.description,
     c.user_concurrent_program_name, d.application_name,
     DECODE(b.request_unit_type,'A','Application',
          decode(b.request_unit_type,'P','Program',
               decode(b.request_unit_type,'S','Req Set', b.request_unit_type))) Type,
     c.concurrent_program_name, b.last_update_date, b.last_updated_by
FROM   fnd_request_groups a,
     FND_REQUEST_GROUP_UNITS b,
     fnd_concurrent_programs_vl c,
     fnd_application_tl d,
     fnd_application_tl e
WHERE  a.request_group_id = b.request_group_id
AND    b.request_unit_id = c.concurrent_program_id
AND    a.application_id = e.application_id
AND    b.unit_application_id = d.application_id
AND    b.request_unit_type = 'P'
-- Variables that can be utilized for tracking.
--AND    a.request_group_name = 'All Reports'
--AND    e.application_name = 'Oracle Payables'
--AND    c.user_concurrent_program_name = 'Mass Additions Create Report'
--AND    e.application_id = 20001  -- Our Payables = 20001
ORDER BY a.request_group_name,
       e.application_name,
       c.user_concurrent_program_name ;
```

Query 10b: Request sets contained in Request Groups

```
SELECT a.request_group_name, e.application_name, a.description,
     c.user_request_set_name, d.application_name,
     DECODE(b.request_unit_type,'A','Application',
          decode(b.request_unit_type,'P','Program',
               decode(b.request_unit_type,'S','Req Set', b.request_unit_type))) TYPE,
     c.request_set_name, b.last_update_date, b.last_updated_by
FROM   fnd_request_groups a,
     FND_REQUEST_GROUP_UNITS b,
     fnd_request_sets_vl c,
     fnd_application_tl d,
     fnd_application_tl e
WHERE  a.request_group_id = b.request_group_id
AND    b.request_unit_id = c.request_set_id
AND    a.application_id = e.application_id
AND    b.unit_application_id = d.application_id
AND    b.request_unit_type = 'S'
```

```
-- Variables that can be utilized for tracking.
--AND    b.request_unit_id = 1244
--AND    a.request_group_name = 'All Reports'
--AND    e.application_name = 'Oracle Payables'
--AND    c.user_request_set_name = 'GMS: AP Holds - Set'
--AND    e.application_id = 20001 -- Our Payables = 20001
ORDER BY a.request_group_name, e.application_name, c.user_request_set_name ;
```

Query 10c "Application" type entries in Request Groups

```
SELECT a.request_group_name, e.application_name, a.description,
       d.application_name UNIT_APP,
       DECODE(b.request_unit_type,'A','Application',
           decode(b.request_unit_type,'P','Program',
                  decode(b.request_unit_type,'S','Req Set', b.request_unit_type)))
           TYPE,
       b.last_update_date, b.last_updated_by
FROM   fnd_request_groups a,
       FND_REQUEST_GROUP_UNITS b,
       fnd_application_tl d,
       fnd_application_tl e
WHERE  a.request_group_id = b.request_group_id
AND    a.application_id = e.application_id
AND    b.unit_application_id = d.application_id
AND    b.request_unit_type = 'A'
-- Variables that can be utilized for tracking.
--AND    a.request_group_name = 'All Reports'
--AND    d.application_name = 'Oracle Payables'
--AND    e.application_id = 20001  -- Our Payables = 20001
ORDER BY a.request_group_name, e.application_name ;
```

Query 10d: Definition of Request Sets

```
SELECT rs.user_request_set_name
,      rs.request_set_name
,      rs.start_date_active
,      rs.end_date_active
,      rss.stage_name
,      rss.display_sequence
,      rss.description
,      cp.concurrent_program_name
,      cp.user_concurrent_program_name
,      rsp.sequence
FROM   fnd_request_sets_vl      rs
,      fnd_request_set_stages_vl rss
,      fnd_request_set_programs  rsp
,      fnd_concurrent_programs_vl cp
WHERE  rss.set_application_id = rs.application_id
AND    rss.request_set_id = rs.request_set_id
AND    rsp.set_application_id = rss.set_application_id
AND    rsp.request_set_id = rss.request_set_id
```

```
AND    rsp.request_set_stage_id = rss.request_set_stage_id
AND    cp.application_id = rsp.program_application_id
AND    cp.concurrent_program_id = rsp.concurrent_program_id
ORDER BY 1,6,10;
```

Chapter 38: Query 11: Users outside of Password Expiration Policy

Purpose of the Query

The purpose of this query is to identify Users outside of the organization's password expiration policy (i.e. how many days before a User's password needs to be changed). This query supports audit test OV-18.

Note: Update the highlighted value (90) with the password expiration days policy for your organization

Evaluation of results
Sample data from Query 11: Password Expiration Policy Violations

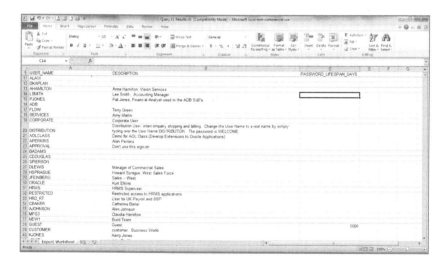

In these query results, you should inquire about each record. Why do User accounts ALAW, DKAPLAN, AHAMILTON, etc. have no PASSWORD_LIFESPAN_DAYS (aka password expiration days)? Why does GUEST have a value of 5,000? Are these permissible considering your corporate policy?

Ask your security administrators to justify why the Users returned in this query don't meet your corporate policy.
Typical recommendations related to the result of this query would be:

1. Manually set the Password Expiration Days through the Users form
2. Have your development team develop a script to update the Password Expiration Days (and call the appropriate public API to make the update).
3. Automate the defaulting of the password expiration value by using forms personalization. See specifications for how to do this at the Book Resources page at www.erpa.net.

Query 11: Users outside of password expiration policy

```
Select user_name, description, password_lifespan_days, end_date
From fnd_user
Where end_date is null
        And (password_lifespan_days is null or password_lifespan_days <> 90)
```

Chapter 39: Query 12: High Risk Single Functions

Purpose of the Query

Purpose: This query identifies the Users and Responsibilities that can access high risk single Functions. This query supports multiple audit tests through this book.

This query is taken from Oracle's MOS Note 403537.1. I have added a significant number of Functions to this query to evaluate additional risks. For the full query (with all the Functions necessary) please refer to the Book Resources page which can be accessed at www.erpra.net.

The limitation of this query is that it does not take into account menu or function exclusions that may be applied at the Responsibility level. Following is an example of Responsibility where a Menu Exclusion is applied:

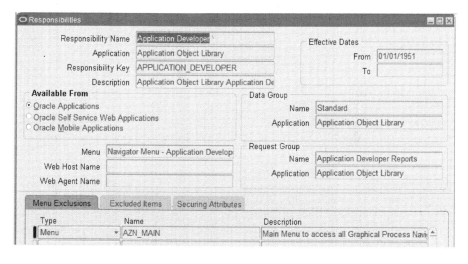

Following is an example of Responsibility where a Function Exclusion is applied:

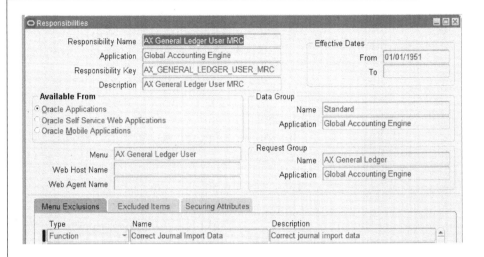

If a Menu Exclusion is applied the entire submenu is not available, including each of the Functions within it.

If a Function Exclusion is applied that Function is not available regardless of how many times it may be present in one or more of the submenus related to the Responsibility's main Menu.

Therefore, the information in this query has to be reviewed along with the information in Query 1 which provides the definition of Responsibilities and Menu and Function exclusions applied. See that chapter above for more information on this topic.

Evaluation of results
Sample data from Query 12: High Risk Single Functions

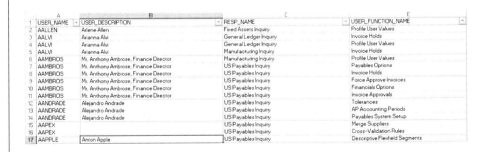

	A USER_NAME	B USER_DESCRIPTION	C RESP_NAME	E USER_FUNCTION_NAME
1	USER_NAME	USER_DESCRIPTION	RESP_NAME	USER_FUNCTION_NAME
2	AALLEN	Arlene Allen	Fixed Assets Inquiry	Profile User Values
3	AALVI	Arianna Alvi	General Ledger Inquiry	Invoice Holds
4	AALVI	Arianna Alvi	General Ledger Inquiry	Profile User Values
5	AALVI	Arianna Alvi	Manufacturing Inquiry	Invoice Holds
6	AAMBROS	Mr. Anthony Ambrose, Finance Director	Manufacturing Inquiry	Profile User Values
7	AAMBROS	Mr. Anthony Ambrose, Finance Director	US Payables Inquiry	Payables Options
8	AAMBROS	Mr. Anthony Ambrose, Finance Director	US Payables Inquiry	Invoice Holds
9	AAMBROS	Mr. Anthony Ambrose, Finance Director	US Payables Inquiry	Force Approve Invoices
10	AAMBROS	Mr. Anthony Ambrose, Finance Director	US Payables Inquiry	Financials Options
11	AAMBROS	Mr. Anthony Ambrose, Finance Director	US Payables Inquiry	Invoice Approvals
12	AANDRADE	Alejandro Andrade	US Payables Inquiry	Tolerances
13	AANDRADE	Alejandro Andrade	US Payables Inquiry	AP Accounting Periods
14	AANDRADE	Alejandro Andrade	US Payables Inquiry	Payables System Setup
15	AAPEX		US Payables Inquiry	Merge Suppliers
16	AAPEX		US Payables Inquiry	Cross-Validation Rules
17	AAPPLE	Anton Apple	US Payables Inquiry	Descriptive Flexfield Segments

Query 12: High risk single Functions

```
select distinct fu.user_name user_name,fu.description user_description,
fr.responsibility_name resp_name,fff.function_name,fff.user_function_name,
fff.description, ff.form_name, ff.user_form_name
from applsys.fnd_user fu,
apps.fnd_user_resp_groups furg,
apps.fnd_responsibility_vl fr,
applsys.fnd_compiled_menu_functions fcmf,
apps.fnd_form_functions_vl fff,
apps.fnd_form_vl ff
where fff.form_id=ff.form_id
and furg.responsibility_id = fr.responsibility_id
and furg.responsibility_application_id = fr.application_id
and fr.menu_id = fcmf.menu_id
and fcmf.grant_flag = 'Y'
and fcmf.function_id = fff.function_id
and furg.user_id = fu.user_id
and sysdate between fu.start_date and nvl(fu.end_date, sysdate+1)
and sysdate between fr.start_date and nvl(fr.end_date, sysdate+1)
and fff.function_name in (
select fun.function_name
from apps.fnd_form_functions_vl fun, apps.fnd_form_vl form
where fff.function_name in (
'AP_POXACCWO'
,'FND_FNDPOMPV'
,'FND_FNDPOMPO')
and fun.form_id=form.form_id)
order by 1,2
```

Chapter 40: Query 13: Password patch

Purpose of the Query

The purpose of this query is to identify whether or not the process to change to Hashed passwords as described in MOS Note 457166.1 has been completed. This query supports audit test OV-1.

Evaluation of results
Sample data from Query 13: Password Patch

	A	B	C	D
1				
2				
3				
4				
5	WARNING:Hashed passwords are not on			
6				

If the result of the script is 'WARNING: Hashed password patch not installed' then you have a finding. If not, there is no finding.

SQL Query: Password Patch

```
Note: this query is provided by Oracle as part of MOS Note 403537.1
REM -----------------------------------------------------------------------
REM
REM run as APPS (really <FNDNAM>)
REM Usage: SQL> @EBSCheckHashedPasswords.sql
REM
REM This script will check the status of Hashed Passwords for Application Users
REM
REM See the E-Business Suite Secure Configuration Guide section
REM Oracle E-Business Suite Security > Authentication > Switch to Hashed
Passwords
REM for more information
REM
REM -----------------------------------------------------------------------
set serveroutput on
declare
  l_status varchar2(50);
begin
dbms_output.put_line('Password Mode');
dbms_output.put_line('--------------------------------------');
execute immediate 'select decode(FND_WEB_SEC.GET_PWD_ENC_MODE,
             null,"WARNING:Hashed passwords are not on",
```

```
                    "Hashed passwords are on") from dual'
into l_status;
dbms_output.put_line(l_status);
exception
 when others then
 if sqlcode=-904 then
  l_status:='WARNING: Hashed password patch not installed';
 else
  l_status:='Unexpected Error';
 end if;
 dbms_output.put_line(l_status);
end;/
```

Appendix A: Terminology

1. ERP System – systems that have distinct application and database layers such as SAP, PeopleSoft, JD Edwards, and Oracle E-Business Suite.

2. ACH – Automated Clearing House which is a United States standard for submitting files electronically to a bank to make payments electronically

3. System Administration – can mean either OS administration or application administration. Will distinguish between the two throughout the book, but generally will refer to the application administration function.

4. SQL – structured query language - SQL is a programming language for querying and modifying data and managing databases.

5. Materiality – According to the SEC, Materiality is "A matter is "material" if there is a substantial likelihood that a reasonable person would consider it important."

6. Sub-material fraud – fraud committed that is less than material – that is the sum of which doesn't rise to the level of 'materiality' as defined by the organization's external auditors. An auditor would argue that a financial statement audit is not designed to identify immaterial fraud, just material fraud.

7. Financial statement audit – an audit of an organization's financial statements (in contrast to an audit of an organization's internal controls as is required by SOX)

8. Internal controls audit - the audit required under section 404 of section as to the design and effectiveness of internal controls (disregarding the intricacies of requirements under PCAOB's AS2 versus those under AS5)

9. COSO – According to Wikipedia[1], Committee of Sponsoring Organizations of the Treadway Commission (COSO) is a U.S.

private-sector initiative, formed in 1985. Its major objective is to identify the factors that cause fraudulent financial reporting and to make recommendations to reduce its incidence. COSO has established a common definition of internal controls, standards, and criteria against which companies and organizations can assess their control systems.

10. Professional forms – example:

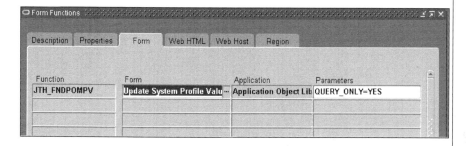

11. OA framework pages – example:

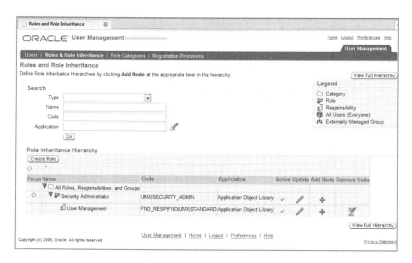

---

[1] http://www.sec.gov/interps/account/sab99.htm

Appendix B: Other Resources

ERP Risk Advisors Hosted Websites

A couple of websites ERP Risk Advisors hosts that have various resources are (all links can be found at www.erpra.net):

- ERP Risk Advisors (www.erpra.net) – our website contains various resources, information about services and training we offer, and links to other valuable information. The website also contains various resources including a soft copy of the queries contained in this book along with a soft copy of the Internal Controls Questionnaire. See the Book Resources page which can be found on the Books page www.erpra.net/books.html.
- Oracle Internal Controls and Security Listserver (http://groups.yahoo.com/group/OracleSox/) – this is a listserver we originally founded in 2004 to discuss Sarbanes-Oxley compliance issues. It has since grown to a discussion forum focused on the broader context of internal controls and security best practices. As a public domain forum, anyone can sign up for membership, including those that want to post via anonymous email accounts such as Gmail, yahoo, and Hotmail. Many organizations have used this forum to ask questions about areas they are struggling without fear of exposing weaknesses about their organization that posting with their work email address would reveal.
- Oracle Apps Internal Controls Repository (http://tech.groups.yahoo.com/group/oracleappsinternalcontrols/) – this is an end-user only, forum. It is open only to end users so that information can be shared without disclosing it to external auditors. I recognize that auditors, like the rest of us, learn about weaknesses and issues within Oracle EBS and other applications in public domain forums. Certain risks and issues are shared in this forum so that end user organizations can address them before auditors become aware. Because membership is restricted to end users, membership requests are only accepted by users that request membership using their work email address. The use of the work email address allows me to verify that the requestor is a member of an end user organization and not an external auditor. Since we also share valuable components of our intellectual property, we

also do not allow other consulting firms or audit firms access to this forum.
- LinkedIn Oracle GRC Group: (http://www.linkedin.com/groups?gid=2017790) – this group facilitates discussion related to Oracle GRC issues among LinkedIn members
- LinkedIn Oracle ERP Auditors: http://www.linkedin.com/groups?gid=2354934) – this group facilities discussion of auditors of ERP systems

Other Websites

Some websites I would recommend are:

- Oracle Applications Users Group (http://www.oaug.org)
  - OAUG is a worthwhile investment for organizations running Oracle EBS.
- Integrigy – (www.integrigy.com) – valuable site for Oracle security resources and software to monitor security risks; including the Password Encryption Risks white paper –http://www.integrigy.com/security-resources/Integrigy_Encrypted_Password_Disclosure.pdf
- Institute of Internal Auditors (www.theiia.org) – The IIA puts out some of the best guidance on best practices in the world. Their Global Technology Audit Guides (GTAG) are a valuable part of my best practices library.
- ISACA – (www.isaca.org)
- ACFE – Association of Certified Fraud Examiners – (www.acfe.com)

Books

Some books I would recommend are:

- Security, Audit & Control Features Oracle E-Business Suite: A Technical and Risk Management Reference Guide, 3rd Edition by Deloitte Touche Tohmatsu Research Team
- From Solution Beacon:
  - The Release 12 Primer: Shining a Light on the Release 12 World
  - The ABCs of Workflow for E-Business Suite Release 11i and Release 12
- Oracle E-Business Suite Financials R12: A Functionality Guide – Mohan Iyer

My Oracle Support Notes

Note Description	Note #
11i: A Guide to Understanding and Implementing SSL for Oracle Applications/Enabling SSL in Release 12	11i: 123718.1 R12: 376700.1
Enabling SSL with Oracle Application Server 10g and the E-Business Suite	340178.1
Encrypting EBS 11i Network Traffic using Advanced Security Option (also for R12)	391248.1
Oracle Applications Credit Card Encryption for 11i	338756.1
Using Transparent Data Encryption (TDE) with the E-Business Suite	11i: 403294.1 R12: 732764.1 R12: 828229.1
Using Oracle Database Vault with Oracle E-Business Suite Releases 11i and 12	950018.1
Configuring Oracle Connection Manager With Oracle E-Business Suite Release 12	558959.1
Overview of Oracle Applications Audit Trails	60828.1
How To Make All The Responsibilities Read Only For A User	363298.1
Security Check List: Steps to Make Your Database Secure from Attacks	131752.1
Page Access Tracking in Oracle Applications Release 12.0	402116.1

Library of Automated Controls in the Oracle eBusiness Suite	278724.1
Script to Check for Default Passwords Being Used for Common Usernames	227010.1
Understanding Data Auditing in Oracle Application Tables	69660.1
Read Only forms allow to update a value when close the form via top right corner 'X'	414069.1

Appendix C: Other Sources of SQL Scripts

- Oracle provides a series of SQL scripts in MOS Note 1334930.1. Check the most recent version of this MOS Note for updates. As of the writing of this book, in the appendix to this document, they provide the following scripts:
    - Check Profile Settings
    - Change Default Passwords
    - Secure APPLSYSPUB
    - Use Secure Flag on DBC File
    - Implement IP address restrictions
    - Migrate to Password Hash
    - Enable Application Tier Secure Socket Layer (SSL)
    - Move Off of Client/Server Components
    - Secure Configuration of Attachments
    - Turn on ModSecurity
    - Encrypt Credit Card Data
    - Separation of Duties: Review Access To "Sensitive Administrative Pages"

    See this document for more details as to the objectives of these SQL scripts